# Celluloid
# and
# Symbols

# CELLULOID
# and
# SYMBOLS

JOHN C. COOPER
and
CARL SKRADE

FORTRESS PRESS
Philadelphia

*Library of Congress Catalog Card Number 70-116461*

2668A70     Printed in U.S.A.     1-138

# Contents

# Preface

As John Calvin stated in the opening sentences of his *Institutes of the Christian Religion,* "our wisdom, insofar as it ought to be deemed true and solid wisdom, consists almost entirely of two parts: the knowledge of God and of ourselves." That is, meaningful theological talk is centered around the question of God and the question of man. But for many, many people of our time, it is precisely between these two questions that the chasm has developed.

This chasm would seem to have developed out of a vast complex of factors, more factors than we need to go into here for they have been carefully chronicled and catalogued by many writers. However, factors which seem to have been of particular importance in this development are such things as (1) the Scientific Revolution and the Enlightenment, which served to focus attention on the question of man and went on to talk in most optimistic terms of his abilities and possibilities, and (2) a half century of tragic global conflict, including Auschwitz and Hiroshima and, now, Vietnam, which has effectively canceled out optimism by forcing men to peer into the abyss, to realize that not only the hope of meaning in life but even life per se is threatened.

The church has generally sought to answer the questions posed to it both by the old optimism and the new pessimism by withdrawal to a set of stock answers clustered around its old "God-symbols," symbols which the church claims to hold in trust as guardian of "Book" and/or "Tradition." All too often, these symbols have proven unintelligible to those who have focused (optimistically or pessimistically) on the question of man. That is, the church has held on to its old symbols while many, perhaps most, in our culture have moved on from one form of talk about man to another with the resulting gap between church and man at large—a gap which is painfully obvious in our time, both in terms of externals such as a downward dip in church attendance statistics and in terms of the increasingly apparent irrelevance of the church in the lives of men.

While many might argue that those who ignore the church can well afford to do so, the church and its theologians cannot pose the counterargument that the church can afford to ignore society at large, for certainly a primary reason for the church's existence— now as always—is to minister to society. Now as always, the church must seek to be servant to *this* world. Therefore, the church must take up with renewed vigor the question of man, the other basic pole of the search for "true and solid wisdom."

In their consideration of such matters as the question of man and the why of the death of the old symbols and the whence of new symbols, theologians have turned increasingly to the contemporary arts. Thus, for example, over the past thirty years we have seen the emergence of theology and literature as a field in which one may obtain a degree. It would seem that there has been this turning to the arts because it is the belief of many that these arts form a natural bridge between church and society. Further, these arts may not only afford some explanations concerning the reasons for the death of the old symbols but may also contain with them sources for the rebirth of old symbols and/or the birth of new symbols which may speak effectively of and to man in our time.

It is within this general context that we offer this anthology of essays on theology and the cinema. We have chosen to explore the interrelation of theology and the cinema both because of our interest in—perhaps, better, our affection for—the cinema, and because we feel that the most live and vital and significant of the contemporary arts are to be found in the cinema. We feel that the cinema is that art which speaks most effectively of and to man in our time.

This volume is most modest in its intention. We wish only to probe the interrelation of theology and films; we are more interested in raising questions than offering answers. Secondly, we wish to emphasize that we feel that theology needs to be *in dialogue* with the cinema but must never regress to a monologue which would seek to "baptize" the film-maker or impose any kind of theology on him. If in any sense we live in a world come of age, the theologian must speak with other men, not at them.

We wish to give our thanks to the many individuals, named and unnamed, who have made this volume possible. In particular, we wish to thank these men who have so selflessly contributed their essays to this volume: Father William Lynch, S.J., Writer-in-Residence at St. Peter's College in New Jersey, whose essay underlines the necessity of critical analysis of both form and content of contemporary films; we extend our thanks also to Commonweal Publishing Company for their permission to publish Father Lynch's essay. James Wall, Editor of *The Christian Advocate,* who writes on the biblical spectaculars and their appeal—or lack thereof—for people today. William Hamilton of New College, who examines the death of the old symbols as is evidenced by the films of Bergman and Polanski. Harvey Cox of Harvard Divinity School, who probes the purpose of the grotesque in Fellini's films. Robert W. Wagner, Chairman of the Department of Photography and Cinema at Ohio State University and a distinguished film-maker and teacher, who offers his perspectives on the theologians' concern with the cinema. Father Anthony Schillaci, O.P., of the National Film Study Program at Fordham University, who studies the themes of good and evil in the films of Bergman; our thanks also to Fides Publishers, Inc., for their permission to publish Father Schillaci's essay. Robert Jenson of Gettysburg Theological Seminary, who examines the relation of word and Word and image in current cinema. To these men especially we give our gratitude.

The remaining two essays in the book are our own. Skrade's programmatic piece considers possible points of interrelationship of theology and the cinema, and Cooper examines some images of man offered by current cinema.

*Preface*

Quite obviously, the strengths of this book, whatever they may be, are primarily those of our contributors; the weaknesses of the book we must claim for ourselves. Our primary hope for this volume is that it may offer some stimulation for further theological dialogue with the world of the magic shadows on the silver screen which has become such an influential force in our time.

JOHN C. COOPER, PH.D.
*Eastern Kentucky University*
*Richmond, Kentucky*

CARL SKRADE, TH.D.
*Capital University*
*Columbus, Ohio*

January 1970

# Acknowledgments

We are grateful to Fides Publishers, Inc., Notre Dame, Indiana, for permission to republish "Bergman's Vision of Good and Evil" by Anthony Schillaci, which first appeared in *Movies and Morals*.

Portions of William Hamilton's essay appeared under the title "Ingmar Bergman and the Silence of God" in the November 1966 issue of *Motive* magazine. Used by permission.

Father William F. Lynch's essay, "Counterrevolution in the Movies," first appeared in *Commonweal*, October 20, 1967. Used by permission.

# 1

# Theology and Films

Carl Skrade

It has become a commonplace for theologian and nontheologian alike in our time to state and probe the awesome gap which has developed between the church and our society as a whole. As matters stand, increasing numbers of our society see the church not as good or as bad, but simply as irrelevant. This holds true not only for those without church affiliations but also for so many "within" the church who are unable to live out any relation between their "theology" and their real lives; that is, those who can see no meaningful connection between the corner of Sunday morning they may spend in church and the other 99 percent of the week.

Again, as many have noted, an important reason for this state of affairs is the church's inability to perceive just what modern man's questions are. The church has tended to insist that questions be asked and answers given in terms of the traditional forms in Scripture and systematics and symbolics. But there is no reason to expect our Scriptures or our systems or our creeds to be the source of all the religious questions and answers of twentieth-century man; in fact, it seems obvious that these sources cannot even pose all the questions adequately. As Tillich repeatedly reminded us, "in believing they [the churches] had all the answers, they deprived the answers of meaning. These answers were no longer understandable because the questions were no longer understood, and this was the churches' fault. The churches did not ask the questions over again."[1]

How may the church learn to talk in and to the new realities? The possibilities are legion, but within these possibilities certainly the arts are of a particular importance. Art is the reflection of the soul of a culture. While religion is the soul or spirit of culture, it is within its art that a culture may be said to think about itself, pose its questions, probe for answers. Thus, for example, we know of the ancient Sumerians' serene belief in their own supremacy and their humane hope for all mankind from such works as the statues from the Abu Temple at Tell Asmar and the famous stele of Ur-Nammu. The Athenians' love of harmony and freedom is visible in the great works which graced their sacred sites. We read the dreams of the Roman Empire in the busts of the Caesars. Dürer's demons and angels help to lay bare the culture which was the womb for Luther and the Reformation.

If we wish to know the driving concerns of a culture, we may read these concerns by searching into its dominant art forms, by isolating and examining the pervasive factors in its basic arts. In the arts of each age, the age cries out its form of the questions of identity and purpose. Here, in great depth and passionate seriousness, man asks, "What does it mean to be? What am I? Who am I? What are my possibilities? My limitations? Why do I experience satisfaction? Dissatisfaction? What is my *telos* or purpose and goal?" These are among the basic concerns of the art of any age. In our age also the arts probe these questions and seek answers intelligibly in terms of today's setting and language and idioms. Within our arts our culture thinks about itself. Thus, the theologian is rewarded by looking into the arts, for there he can read the fundamental man-questions, obviously one of the basic poles of all meaningful theological talk.

Further, if we ask after the art form which dominates our own period, we cannot answer without a consideration of the cinema. Ours is the age dominated by the moving images and the immediate experience, lights and shadows on a silver screen. The film is the art form which has grown to a maturity in our own era. Further, the film, with its complex intertwining of art and industry, is that art form which may claim the widest exposure; indeed, there is no corner of our society which can escape it. As many have noted, the film is the form which saturates us via cinema and/or TV. For the first time since Gutenberg, we are turned from word-consciousness to consciousness of the visual image. It is to the films that we can, perhaps must, look for the self-interpretation of our period; here we can find our age's "religious" questions, our age's askings about the meaning of existence. Thus my thesis is this: films as a prime locus of contemporary man's questionings concerning the meaning of his existence can serve as the basis for a fruitful dialogue between the church and the world. Pastor and teacher in parish and classroom need to explore the potentials the film offers them in their task.

Now I would not suggest that the questions and answers lie ready at hand in the contemporary film. But an honest examination of films, at the very least, can help us avoid giving first- or seventeenth- or nineteenth-century answers to questions no one is asking. In the films we can find out what questions *are* being asked and how. These films can help us regain, in contemporary form, the basic questions which we affirm Christianity can answer—or at least permit us to live with these questions as we honestly and openly await the answers.

Let me now try to illustrate more concretely what I mean by the religious questions and concerns of contemporary films. Obviously, not all films are of consequence; however, a surprising number do pose basic religious questions. Further, the nature and shape of questions *not* being asked can speak loudly.

First, let us examine the questions of man's situation, or better, his predicament as we find it stated in contemporary films. What do the films have to say concerning man's potentials and his successes or failures in fulfilling these potentials? What do films say or fail to say concerning the reality of evil? For reasons which will become evident as we continue, I would like to probe these questions as they appear in films against the background of some thoughts of the Jewish scholar, Abraham Heschel. Heschel says that questions about evil unavoidably arise "in a civilization where factories were established in order to exterminate millions of men, women, and children; where soap was made of human flesh," but then he goes on to decry the difficulty of discussing evil and the gap between mankind's potentialities and actualities because modern man has become hardened to horror, has lost his sense of horror. Heschel then suggests that modern man at least should be horrified at this loss of a sense of horror.[2]

Both aspects of Heschel's patently religious talk, both the reality that man has lost his sense of horror and the cry that he be horrified at this loss, are evident in at least two current films. I have in mind two "war" films, Robert Aldrich's *The Dirty Dozen* and Richard Lester's *How I Won the War*.[3]

M.G.M. released *The Dirty Dozen* several years ago; since that time it has been smashing box-office records. Its backers believe that it will be, financially speaking, one of the most successful films of all time. The people—the contemporary American people who have difficulty finding the church relevant—like this film; the *Daily News* reported that the New York premiere brought the loudest burst of applause ever heard on Broadway. The reviews have generally been favorable; the critics like it, too.

Finding out what this film says may tell us something about the shape of contemporary man. What this film and its reception do tell us is, I believe, precisely what Heschel claims. We have very nearly lost our sense of horror and thus our ability to distinguish good and evil, our ability to recognize and challenge wrongs.

The story of *The Dirty Dozen* is this: It is the eve of the Normandy invasion. As a measure for enhancing Allied chances for success, someone hatches a scheme for sending a commando unit into Brittany in order to blow up a rest-and-recovery hostel for Nazi officers. A unit is formed for this mission; at its head is a Major Reisman, a challenge to the army's modes and methods, a fly in the military ointment. Under him are a dozen men from a military prison, murderers and the like. Many of them were being held for execution; all have rejected the standards and mores of the military and of society at large. If their mission succeeds, they are to be rewarded with clemency; if it fails, the military establishment has simply been spared the trouble of dealing with them.

The high drama, the irony, the complex play of sympathies we might expect concerning the rightness and wrongness of the men and their mission and of the military philosophy behind it are quickly dissipated. "The suspense is reduced to one simple question: Will the convicts be able to form a spirited team, become devoted and committed to each other and to their mission? We are asked to plug for their reformation, their happy accommodation to military reality."⁴

We never get a glimpse of "the dozen's" criminality; their rebelliousness is quickly channeled to the "good" goal of killing "the enemy." Nor does the film contain any "coherent, controlled awareness of the way in which the military feeds on men's dissatisfaction and animosities for its own purpose. . . . *The Dirty Dozen,* like the military society it pretends to despise, glosses over the grotesque ironies of wartime civilization with plenty of he-man calisthenics and cheery belly laughs."⁵

The climax of the film comes when the German officers and their guests—mostly women—are bottled up in a bomb shelter. As other Germans try to fight them free, the dirty dozen drop grenades, gasoline, and fuses through ventilators down into the shelter. There is here an inevitable reference to the gas chambers; Aldrich admits this. And the film-makers have manipulated us to cheer all this; we accept the cruelty, we are superiors to killers and killed alike. Unlike great art, which can help us acknowledge and analyze our baser impulses (let's face it; battle scenes are generally more exhilarating than depressing), *The Dirty Dozen* simply has us responding "as if we were dogs, with bloodthirsty vehemence and we pretend that this degradation is relaxing, inspiring entertainment."⁶

Only one of the dirty dozen returns alive, but the movie concludes, with a martial air in the background, by intoning, "They died in the line of duty." And the manipulated walk out, a little less concerned about being concerned about the issues behind the

Vietnam conflict (the film really is about this war, not World War II), a little more convinced "that war is lots of gutsy action and a stirring road to manhood and fulfillment," a little more determined that there is no need and/or possibility for challenging authority.[7] *The Dirty Dozen* is both symptomatic of and contributing to contemporary man's loss of the sense of horror.

As one film critic has noted, a good antiwar film is almost impossible.[8] This is so because, in principle, men have already agreed that war is a tragic waste while, in fact, we all have impulses which respond with something less than grief to a good old battle scene. So one might argue that most war films do more to deaden our sense of horror than resurrect it. However, I believe that at least one recent war movie can contribute to the latter. This is Richard Lester's *How I Won the War*. Lester in this film, like Heschel in his theology, asks us the troubling question, "What has become of our sense of horror?"

This film, adapted from Patrick Ryan's book by the same title, follows the adventures of Ernest Goodbody, a young officer who takes part in all the major British campaigns against the Germans in World War II. Goodbody, though bright and concerned with carrying on a man's war for good ends, is, alas, a bungler who leaves his wake of inane accomplishments and broken bodies. This is Lester's cutting edge, his alternation of humor and horror in such fashion that by shock of contrast he breaks us loose from our platitudes, from our "war-is-hell-what-else-is-new" attitude, and asks us to take one more look into the depths of ourselves and our time.

Let me give but one illustration of this juxtaposition of humor and horror which carries the questions in this film. In one scene, a platoon of British soldiers is creeping up on an Italian gasoline dump in North Africa. The Italian sentries spot them, and men on both sides raise their guns—which are jammed. "The resulting tableau is hilarious; but suddenly the guns start to work, and while the audience is still laughing, a soldier is shot in the stomach."[9] Here the shooting is not all part of the fun and games; it wrenches you out of a laugh; it makes you feel uneasy and asks you why you were able to laugh in the first place.

Lester mixes humor and horror in this fashion on up through the film until he has the audience expecting the occasional alternation of humor, a little relief as the film drones home the message that war isn't pretty and there aren't any good guys and nobody wins. But just when the audience has come to expect this relief, Lester takes it away in a bitter, unrelieved scene in which Goodbody's platoon is trapped in a house. German tanks come and shell it, and then the camera follows three of the men in turn as they are tracked down and cornered and killed.

In this fashion, Lester makes his point; no one in the film is either funny or blameless—and we should be horrified that we expect either was possible. In horror, we twentieth-century men must look anew for our lost sense of horror. Only out of a renewed awareness of the void, only out of a renewed awareness of the structures of destruction, can we speak of the possibility of hope. This is what Lester's film drives home to its audiences; the movie is a filmic plea for man to ask after the ancient paths.

Where did man get off the paths? Whence his loss of the sense of horror? What is the origin and genesis of this predicament which modern man experiences? With these questions the contemporary film is concerned.

As a backdrop for the films' concern with these questions, let us use a familiar analysis by Paul Tillich. Tillich says that man in our time has lost his ability to be grasped by an infinite concern, has lost his religious dimension. Why has this dimension, this depth, been lost? Not because of any widespread and rampant impiety in modern man. "Modern man is neither more pious nor more impious than man in any other period. The loss of the dimension of depth is caused by the relation of man to his world and to himself in our period, the period in which nature is being subjected scientifically and technically to the control of man. In this period, life in the dimension of depth is replaced by life in the horizontal dimension. The driving forces of the industrial society of which we are a part go ahead horizontally and not vertically. In popular terms this is expressed in phrases like 'better and better,' 'bigger and bigger,' and 'more and more.' . . .

"If we now ask what does man do and seek if he goes ahead in the horizontal dimension, the answer is difficult. . . . For on his way into space and time man changes the world he encounters. And the changes made by him change himself. He transforms everything he encounters into a tool; and in doing so he himself becomes a tool. But if he asks, a tool for what, there is no answer. . . .

"When in this way man has deprived himself of the dimension of depth . . . , he then becomes a part of the horizontal plane. He loses his self and becomes a thing among things. . . . He becomes an element in the process of manipulated production and manipulated consumption.

"Under these pressures, man can hardly escape the fate of becoming a thing among the things he produces, a bundle of conditioned reflexes without a free, deciding and responsible self. The immense mechanism, set up by man to produce objects for his use, transforms man himself into an object used by the same mechanism of production and consumption."[10]

Now I doubt that the Italian film director Michelangelo Antonioni has ever read a word from Paul Tillich's writings; I have not even found any traces of theological education in Antonioni's biographical sketches. However, I cannot conceive of a more powerful, gripping, unrelenting illustration and experience of Tillich's analysis of the sources and reality of contemporary man's dilemma than Antonioni's *The Red Desert*. Absolutely everything in this film contributes to driving home the same points. His use of camera movements, color, sound, scenery, and character portrayal (or "characterlessness portrayal") all move us to face this reality: twentieth-century man experiences himself as a mechanical and meaningless cog caught up in the machines with which he has habited this industrial wasteland.

Antonioni tells us that the tools and structures of our age have depersonalized us and barely left us with the power to voice our anguish. The ominous ships and machines in *Red Desert* emerge into focus out of fogs and steam and sulfurous fumes which suggest to us the demonic which has eluded human control, and (like

Frankenstein's monster) have taken on a life of their own, are no longer the responsive slaves of their makers. The machines and factories are overwhelmingly large and cacophonously unenduring and they appear about to push the human figures off the borders of the screen.

Man caught up in this meaningless, nightmarish conflict is simply unable to break through the oppression and get to know himself, let alone anyone else. In a particularly disturbing way, the bedroom scenes underline all this. In one scene, six characters lie together on a bed, but they are simply six people alone together, unable to do more than muster a few feeble and unsuccessful attempts to break out of the barrenness and know one another. One has the feeling that a good old-fashioned orgy would be much less immoral. The second bedroom scene, in which the two main characters do engage in the sex act, is a terrible, anguished, unfulfilled cry to know and be known.

The representatives of our age in Antonioni's *Red Desert* are presented, literally, as unfocused in relation to their world, one another, themselves. They are Antonioni's image of man in our century, an image of desolate loneliness, isolation, discontinuity. The relatedness of persons to persons, of persons to the fruitfulness of the earth, is broken, and without these relations, says Antonioni, there is no life.

Let me sum up Antonioni's *Red Desert* with another quote from Tillich:

The essential categories, time, space, causality, substance, have lost their ultimate power. They gave meaning to our world. With their help we could understand things. We could understand that one thing follows the other, one causes the other, one is distinguished from the other, each has its space and its time and so on. . . . But all this no longer applies. Mankind does not feel at home in this world any more. The categories have lost their embracing and overwhelming and asserting power. There is no safety in the world.[11]

Like Psalm 90 and the Book of Job, like Paul Tillich, Antonioni says of man that "his place does not know him anymore." There is no home and no healing, no salvation.

In addition to the development of an industrial society programmed for the horizontal plane, there are, of course, many other factors to be considered in seeking the source of contemporary man's loss of meaning. I would now like to probe what I consider to be another of these factors by examining some examples of that peculiarly American film genre, the Western. The Western is *the* prime American myth, the American dream of righteousness and fulfillment. But the Western myth, however attractive and entertaining, ultimately contains an inadequate analysis of our realities and potentialities. Therefore, it cannot contribute to our healing but can only, insofar as it is believed, abet and increase the predicament of modern man.

In its filmic form, the Western myth dates back to the turn of the century and Edwin S. Porter's *The Great Train Robbery* and Owen Wister's *The Virginian*. The myth has been regarbed and repeated in seemingly countless versions since that time, but perhaps the artistic acme of its expression is Fred Zinnemann's *High Noon*. The Western myth which has been so powerful and influential in shaping the American dream of righteousness is clearly and movingly articulated by Gary Cooper in his role as Marshall Kane. Let's examine the myth in terms of Cooper and this movie.

The hero whom Cooper plays is ahistorical; his past with its involvement with his antagonists and—if there be any—his protagonists is blurred. But we don't need to know about any of this. The film's conflict is basically quite simple; it's simply the good guy versus the bad guys, it's simply virtue versus vices. The virtues are he-manness and outdoorsness and independence; the vices are citified civilization and overstrong scruples and dependence. Shorn of the past, presenting only a unilinear character development, this *High Noon* version of the myth offers none of the complexities of real life. Cooper's major choice is between risking the happiness of his new bride and his own personal integrity, his honor. "There is really no complexity in this; the issues are clearly understood; the lines are clearly drawn; there is not even the question of legal responsibility. . . . His stern will and his honor give him no choice;

he will not run and face the continued threat of violence; he cannot, and be a man, even though his bride attempts to dissuade him with her hysterical fears and her womanish mores. So he goes out into the street and plays out the little drama of the gunfight, in which, inevitably, he is triumphant."[12]

These are the main features of the myth. There is a simple choice between simple good and simple bad and we all know what the difference is; thus the choice to be made is obvious. It is a tribute to the artistry of the film-makers that we can feel any suspense at all, for we know that in the Western myth virtue always triumphs in the end; it simply must. How could it be otherwise?

The Western myth and the American's relation to it is summed up for us in the following statement from Robert Warshow's classic study of this genre:

What he [the cowboy hero] defends, at bottom, is the purity of his own image—in fact, his honor. This is what makes him invulnerable. . . . The Westerner is the last gentleman, and the movies which over and over again tell his story are probably the last art form in which the concept of honor retains its strength. . . . The fact that he continues to hold our attention is evidence enough that, in his proper frame, he presents an image of personal nobility that is still real for us.[13]

For part of our society, I suppose for part of each of us, he is still real, this Western hero. May I suggest that the reality of the myth's power is visible in the Goldwater platform in the 1964 presidential campaign, a platform which saw our whole frighteningly complex modern world in terms of simple goods and simple bads which modern knights on their modern chargers were ready and willing to categorize and conquer for us. Further, isn't the simplistic approach of the Western hero evident in the position of those who would tell us that the war in Vietnam or the riots in the ghettos have simple solutions which are evident to anyone with good intentions? Finally, isn't it a basic claim of fundamentalist theology that it is only those who have been captured or confused by Beelzebub who would question the simple solutions of the "good old-time religion," much of which harks all the way back to the nineteenth-century American frontier?

11

So there is indeed a sense in which the Western myth is still real and powerful among us. However, there is also in our time a radical challenge to the myth. To many in our time, this myth is seen as an inauthentic holdover from a past that never was, a false idealization and oversimplification which can only handicap our attempts to deal with those questions which do close in upon us.

A sharp filmic challenge to the Western myth is to be found in a promising new breed of Western movies. By this I do not mean those films which the distributors are prone to advertise as "adult" Westerns. These "adult" Westerns' general characteristics are some real mud in the streets, a teasing bedroom scene or two to titillate the imagination of our so-called sexy society, and a certain sugges-tion of the futility of heroic action in a nonheroic world. To bor-row a phrase from Karl Jaspers, these films are miseries, not tragedies; since they only play around the edges of important prob-lems, they are ultimately as unsatisfactory and as dangerous as their "Western myth" predecessors.

The filmic challenges to the Western myth have come in such recent movies as Martin Ritt's *Hud* and *The Outrage* and *Hombre,* in Burt Kennedy's *Welcome to Hard Times,* and in John Huston's *The Misfits.* Let's look at the challenge in terms of *The Misfits* and *Hombre.*

Like *High Noon, The Misfits* presents its story in terms of the Western setting; unlike *High Noon, The Misfits*'s approach to life is not simplistic but complex; i.e., it tries to get much closer to actuality. In *The Misfits,* the cowboy, Gay (Clark Gable), pre-sents us with a sharp and explicit contrast to the myth, "for though he uses the cowboy myth as his way of life, and stumbles from failure to failure in pursuit of it, shouting defiance in the face of inevitable change, the mythic criteria of absolute independence and virile, physical masculinity on which he shapes his life are the forces which have made him a failure, since they are of little use in truly coping with any real world. . . ." Gay fails precisely because he believes the myth. He and all his companions are "mis-fits in the sense that they seek to live outside of history in an enchanted land of dreams. In the end, there is the realization that not only is there no place for the cowboy—the image of the natural man—in the contemporary society, there never *was* a place for him, except on its fringes, where he could neither define it nor benefit from it. The dream he dreamed was excessively romantic; the fact that he believed in it made him impossibly so."[14] *The Misfits,* with its disturbing actuality, seeks to voice a message quite similar to the haunting homelessness of *The Red Desert.*

*Hombre,* visually, is even closer to *The Red Desert.* Martin Ritt's West is a place of decay. This is evident in the very settings used in the film. "The boardinghouse is closing down, and so is the stagecoach office. The relay station along the road has already closed, though one man remains there, with nothing to do. And the deserted mine—empty buildings, dust, piles of rocks, absolute silence—where the driver stops early in the journey, and where the final clash takes place, is an evocative, lingering visual image of stagnation. The world Ritt portrays is the West dying."[15]

The leading character of this film, Russell, is played by Paul Newman; the role has a number of similarities to Newman's part in another Ritt movie, *Hud.* Russell hardly fits the cowboy-hero stereotype; he is a hard and bitter and skeptical man who makes us ask anew what makes a good act good and what makes a courageous act courageous. To paraphrase Koheleth, he is not righteous overmuch and he does not make himself overwise (Eccles. 7:16). He sees an evil in all that is done under the sun and knows that one fate comes to all (Eccles. 9:3); he knows this and doesn't expect more. In the end he does make the noble gesture, perhaps because he, too, has come to believe that "if two lie together, they are warm" (Eccles. 4:11), but that certainly one cannot be warm alone. But Russell dies painfully, even without the heroine's kiss. Unlike Marshall Kane, he doesn't tell us that there are noble and ready-made answers which we can plug into at will, if we are men of good will. However, he does ask us anew those questions which can be seriously asked only out of an awareness of the dimension of depth. Russell calls us into a consideration of actualities, not of false dreams, not of myths.

13

As I have tried to show, it seems certain that contemporary films can aid us and our society in the rediscovery of "the basic questions to which the Christian symbols are the answers"[16] in a way which is understandable to our time. One further question which I would like to consider is this: Can films go beyond the gloomy questions, beyond analyzing the predicament? The films discussed thus far obviously serve primarily to accentuate and articulate the negative. What of the positive? Of what positive value are films in the face of the awesome questions?

First, as I have been implying above, I think films have great possibilities for assisting us to see and face the real, no matter how unpleasant that reality is. Certainly the contemporary film has positive values if it speaks to us in an understandable way about the basic questions we face as persons, questions about who we are, why we are here, and what it means to live responsibly as men and women in the world today.

What Martin Esslin has said about the religious function of the Theatre of the Absurd holds true also for many contemporary films. Any honest effort, "however timid and tentative, to sing, to laugh, to weep—and to growl—if not in praise of God, at least in search of a dimension of the Ineffable; any effort to make man aware of the ultimate realities of his condition, to instill in him again the lost sense of cosmic wonder and primeval anguish, to shock him out of an existence that has become trite, mechanical, complacent, and deprived of the dignity that comes of awareness" is of positive value.[17] One might also add that the film is much more effective in this task than is the theater because the film possesses much more vitality than the theater in our time. Further, the film reaches a much larger audience; it talks to more people.

Perhaps this is the primary contribution of the films, this serious and honest examination of the sacred void; perhaps such honest waiting and watching is more important for our moment than anything else. Perhaps the "symbols of glory" are without adequate filmic representation. However, "no premature solutions should be tried; rather, the human situation in its conflicts should be expressed courageously. If it is expressed, it is already transcended: He who can express guilt shows that he already knows about 'acceptance-in-spite-of.' He who can bear and express meaninglessness shows that he experiences meaning within his desert of meaninglessness."[18] Perhaps there is within the anguish of a *Red Desert* an awareness of an "acceptance-in-spite-of" which is itself a rebirth.

Second, I think films have great positive potential in that they can help us to break down the walls between the sacred and the secular, can help us realize once again that "the whole world is God's monastery." Reference to a couple of classical studies of the theory of film can perhaps help to make this point. In Bela Balazs's *Theory of Film,* a work originally published in the 1920s, there is a chapter entitled "The Faces of Men." Here Balazs argues that since the invention of printing the visual world has been relegated to a position of secondary importance; words, conceptualizations have taken over. Balazs believed that filmic procedures will cause us to develop a renewed awareness and renewed affirmation of our concrete, visible, and visual world, the immediate worth of which he portrays in almost Hebraic terms.[19]

The second work which I have in mind is Siegfried Kracauer's *Theory of Film,* a book with the suggestive subtitle "The Redemption of Physical Reality." It is Kracauer's contention that the film should explore the given, visible, physical world because he believes that the depths of meaning are *within* these realities, not in the conceptualizations we force down on top of reality. The film-maker is to set out to explore physical data and, taking his cue from it, work his way up to some belief or problem, not vice versa. Kracauer quotes Dekeukeleire's statement: "If the senses exert an influence on our spiritual life, the cinema becomes a powerful ferment of spirituality by augmenting the number and quality of our sense perceptions."[20] Kracauer and Balazs call on us to behold, via films, the world; the theologian would add "which thou hast made."

Haig P. Manoogian in his excellent book, *The Film-Maker's Art,* quotes John Ruskin's statement that "the greatest thing a human soul ever does in this world is to see something, and tell what it saw in a plain way. Hundreds of people can talk for one who can think but thousands can think for one who can see. To see clearly is poetry, prophecy and religion, all in one."[21] It is justifiable to place this quote in a book on film study, for films do hold the potential of helping us to develop eyes that see the visible, physical realities as that which God has given.

However, eyes that see films discerningly do not just happen; the appreciation and understanding of film (or any other art) is something which most of us have to learn. In view of our age's saturation with the filmic, there is an undeniable need for screen education. A glance at some statistics can help to underline this need:

By the time a typical American student graduates from high school today, he has watched some 15,000 hours of television and has seen more than 500 films. The TV figure is the result of an average of twenty hours weekly viewing for fifteen years, adding up to two full years of 24-hour-a-day televiewing. During the same period of time, this average student has attended school five hours a day, 180 days per year, for twelve years, to produce a total of 10,800 hours of school time. Only sleeping time surpasses television [i.e., film at home] as a top time-consumer.[22]

As Father Culkin, G. William Jones, and others have said, a ministry to the whole of the twentieth-century man can scarcely avoid the task of helping people to understand better what they see on the screen; Jones's own suggestions for procedures are invaluable. Thus, a third positive potential of the serious study of films within the parish or the religion curriculum of a college or university is the opportunity this affords for helping people better understand and evaluate a very basic and influential aspect of twentieth-century existence. The film can become an increasingly valuable factor in learning and doing, not just escaping.

A fourth value of the study of films within parish or classroom rests in the potential which films have for overcoming communication barriers. To use G. William Jones's term, the screen is "a communication block-buster." Jones states:

If we can learn to utilize the screen as a source of contemporary parables, then our process of Christian witness and education can become less a matter of saying, "This is what life means. Take it or leave it," and more a matter of saying, "This is what life looks like. What do you make of it?" The virtue of this second approach is that in the viewer's act of extracting the truth from the screen narrative, and formulating and expressing it for himself in group discussion, the truth will become *his* truth and not just a string of words which he has accepted from someone else.[23]

A fifth possible value of the film is the potential which it holds for examining and proclaiming the gospel. I do not mean that the analyses of the human predicament and the questions which are asked in caustic form in such films as *How I Won the War* or *The Red Desert* or *The Misfits* or *Hombre* in and of themselves contain Christian answers. The value of these films is that they are a powerful renewal of the questions which themselves have been lost by much traditional theology. However, these films remain questions, not answers. As Tillich has said, "the answer cannot be derived from the question. It is said *to* him who asks, but it is not taken from him. The Church has the function of answering the question . . . of the meaning of this existence. [The task of the Church] is to show to the people outside the Church that the symbols in which the life of the Church expresses itself are answers to the question implied in their very existence as human beings."[24]

The questions are not themselves the answers. Also, the grand certainties of some previous eras are behind us and we have no evidence of their imminent resurrection. However, is it true that our age is without its own symbols of renewal with their message of healing? In fact, may it not be that such symbols are to be found within some of our contemporary films? I believe that some of our contemporary films do contain such affirmations of the possibilities of affirmations in the midst of the emptiness of our times. Let me cite two filmic examples.

Antonioni's recent film is the difficult and provocative *Blow-up*, a film which apparently only latent Victorianism kept from receiving the top National Council of Churches film award for 1967. Yet in many ways this film is as bitter and cheerless and desperate as

*Red Desert.* Where in this meandering nonstory of a London society photographer's experience of the void is there anything remotely resembling a "symbol of renewal"?

The film proceeds through the character of the photographer, who, like other Antonioni characters, is something of a personification of the twentieth-century man's experience of estrangement. He always is at least once removed from involvement; he sees things only through viewfinder and lens. What he sees, whether it be the fashion models with whom he works in his profession or the candid subjects he photographs more as an avocation, are things to be manipulated for his own ends. There are other people around him (one would hesitate to call them friends) but all of the usual commitments are lacking (there is a "wife" who is not really his wife; there are children but they don't have children). There is in this film, as in Antonioni's others, an overwhelming, crushing sense of the void.

However, things change. In a verdant, misty setting in a quiet park, the photographer takes some candid shots of a young girl with an older man, apparently on their way to quiet seclusion. The girl spots the photographer, pursues him in quest of the photos, and ultimately, in his studio, offers her body in return for the film. The photographer is curious about her frightened quest for this film so as soon as he is alone he develops and examines it. Feeling that something is amiss in the whole matter, he is led to make a series of enlargements of a couple of shots. Finally, in an attempt to grasp what it is that he has witnessed, he takes a picture of an enlargement and then enlarges that. Twice removed from reality, the picture so enlarged that it is a coarse and grainy blur, there is visible a phantom image in the park shrubbery; the image is pointing a gun at the girl's male companion.

At this point, late at night, the photographer returns to the park and there discovers amidst the dark and quiet greenness a paled and eerie corpse. The photographer now, for the first time, has a one-to-one direct encounter with a reality, the reality of death. He who for whom all things have been empty is indelibly altered by this involvement with the ultimate emptiness, death.

From this point, the film moves quite rapidly to its close. The photographer goes through a sequence of events that underline the emptiness and death all about him; the difference is that now he cannot acquiesce to this. Whereas previously his attitude was simply that all things have been empty, so what?, now he knows that not all is emptiness. It is not nothing that a man dies; it is something, even though this something is not defined. But there is no external support for his new knowledge of reality; the girl is gone, his photographic record of the event is gone, his "friends" do not understand, and, on his return to the park, even the corpse itself is gone. If he is indeed to be a "new man" he must learn this newness in fear and trembling.

The strange, unforgettable closing scene suggests that this is possible. As he is leaving the park, there comes lurching up a carload of ragged but lively clowns. Their party descends on the tennis court where two of their members take up a match—sans rackets or balls. Their party watches in interest, the photographer also pauses. The make-believe ball is batted back and forth until it is accidently knocked out over the fence of the court. The photographer is the closest person to it; the players motion for him to retrieve it. He does so; the imaginary ball is back in the game; the game resumes—with a single difference. Though we still cannot see a ball, we do hear it, "like the sound of one hand clapping."[25] For him who has become engaged, this is the assurance of things hoped for, the conviction of things not seen.

It is certainly a spare symbol of renewal set amidst the mountains of decay which Antonioni offers us. The camera work and the color emphasize for us just how fragile the hope and how awesome the odds. But within the weak and blotchy greenness which we view from the aerial shot in the final scene, in spite of all, we "feel" a glimpse of new growth.

A second filmic example of hope of renewal in the midst of decay is *Cool Hand Luke*. The first full-length feature by Stuart Rosenberg, whom we have met formerly as the director of the often excellent television series, "The Defenders," *Luke* has not exactly received the total endorsement of the critics. While the

critics generally see promise in the film, many have had reserva-
tions, both for technical reasons and because they feel that the
Christian symbolism is too obvious. However, while the symbolism perhaps has been too heavy-handed for the sophisticated, it has
also been rather offensive for those who maintain that some things
*are* sacred.

Luke (Paul Newman) is a thirtyish ex–war hero in a Southern
town. Hard times and a disdain for the establishment and an over-
dose of firewater have Luke out busting heads off the local parking
meters as the film begins. The result is a rather stiff sentence to a
road gang. It is within the setting of the rigors of this camp that
Luke takes shape as a filmic symbol of renewal. It is Luke who
brings the others at least to the verge of seeing themselves and still
seeing some reason for being.

Luke is the "hasid" (pious man) as the hasid is defined by
Rabbi Bunam of Przyscha. According to medieval sources, a hasid
is he who does more than the law requires. Now this is the law:
Thou shalt not deceive thy fellowman (Lev. 25:17). A hasid,
Rabbi Bunam says, goes beyond the law; he will not even deceive
his own self. Luke sees things as they are, himself, his fellow
inmates, the authorities, and this honesty without malice becomes
a source of new being for all who will accept it, even on their
own terms.

The prime antagonist of Luke is an empty, emotionless overseer
in the camp whose ever present dark glasses have led the inmates
to dub him "No-eyes." No-eyes is a powerful filmic image of non-
being; his capacities for sensitivity have totally atrophied. He is
alone, apart, estranged, dehumanized, a threat to all that is
human, the inexorable black angel. A second antagonist is the
man in charge of the camp. He is more pathetic than No-eyes,
more of a caricature of the human than a personification of the
nonhuman. It is he who reiterates, "What we got here is a failure
of communication," when a prisoner fails to knuckle under and
accept the system.

Luke, as the honest bearer of the meaninglessness of the others,
guards and inmates alike, becomes the bearer of meaning and

purpose. He brings a reason for being, and he does so in no small measure by rejecting the traditional religious reasons. His unsuccessful attempts to escape from the system serve to underline this until he is beaten and broken by the guards, despised and rejected by the inmates. Even this he bears and uses for his final attempt at escape. After an unwitting betrayal by a bullish admirer, he is at last brought down in the house of the God who has forsaken him, truer to this God in his defiance of him than all others who have given Him a false and meaningless lip service. Luke's parting shot at the authorities who ring his prison-church is, "What we got here is a failure to communicate." But Luke is the one who has communicated above all others. He has communicated to friend and foe; this is why, inevitably, he must be removed. Luke is the one who has brought home the meaninglessness and made possible a meaning; he is the filmic Christ-figure par excellence.

In these brief and sketchy summaries of these two films, I believe that there is evidence that the filmic media not only can talk meaningfully about modern man's predicament but also can break through the surface of our illusions and disillusions and can, via the grammar peculiar to the film, force a new consideration of the possibilities of renewal. Certainly, consciously or unconsciously, contemporary film-makers force their audiences not only to examine the structures of destruction and peer into the depths of the human predicament, but they also offer filmic forms of symbols of renewal. Perhaps these artists can minister to us all by breaking through into the realm out of which symbols are born. Perhaps they can not only help us to hear intelligibly those questions to which the Christian gospel has traditionally been the answer, but also can help us renew our vocabulary for speaking those answers. This possibility that they can help us break through to a level of reality which we might otherwise never reach calls for us to listen to them most seriously.

There is one final thought which I must note. Though I have implied it previously, I wish to state it explicitly. In a study of theology and films, the purpose and method of the theologian must not be to force down on top of the world of films theological ways

21

of thinking and talking, let alone theological solutions. There would be something basically dishonest and thus unfruitful in any attempt to "use" the films as a propaganda device for mouthing warmed-over formulas. Rather, if the study of theology and films is to be of any value in our attempts to reunite the God-question and the man-question, the church and the world, both the discipline of theology and the art of the cinema must be allowed their freedom. Instead of returning to some form of monologue in which theology would preach to cinema—or vice versa—both the discipline and the art must be allowed to speak their piece; that is, the goal must be dialogue. "Too often our ability to 'receive' the meaning of an artist's work is jeopardized by our desire to 'use' it. To be grasped by the depth dimension in a work of art, to be open to the ultimate meaning in a penultimate form, demands that we be willing to let it work on us, move us, upset us, rather than to ask how we can use it, what it illustrates, or what point we can make with it."[20] Only within the context of genuine dialogue between theology and films can there be a real possibility of closing the gap between the church and society.

I suspect that one would find a close correlation between good films (i.e., films which are honest in method and intent as they probe reality) and good theology (i.e., a theology which is somewhat successful in its efforts to bring us honestly to understand and face our reality). If the theologian does not try to "use" it, a good film may serve to renew his theology, at least in its apologetic task.

In conclusion, I offer this plea. There is something profane about much of what we do in our college religion classrooms. While we certainly do not intend to do so, we lose students in our talk about lists of Israel's kings and the problems of authorship in the Pastorals and the factors affecting the reception of religion on the American frontier and the nature and attributes of God. Films have "the virtue of being alive and the grace to wonder out loud."[21] Isn't the time ripe for us as theologians both to learn and to teach through dialogue with films?

# NOTES

1. Paul Tillich, "Existentialist Aspects of Modern Art," in *Christianity and the Existentialists,* ed. Carl Michalson (New York: Charles Scribner's Sons, 1956), p. 146.

2. Abraham Heschel, *Man Is Not Alone* (New York: Farrar and Strauss, 1952), p. 11.

3. The films in this essay are referred to under the name of the director involved.

4. Stephen Farber, review of *The Dirty Dozen, Film Quarterly* 21, no. 2 (Winter 1967/68): 37.

5. Ibid., p. 39.

6. Ibid., p. 40.

7. Ibid. I am much indebted to Stephen Farber for his perceptive insights into films and culture, particularly as these insights are spelled out in his *Film Quarterly* articles on *The Dirty Dozen* and *Hombre.*

8. William Johnson, "Shooting at Wars," ibid., p. 31.

9. Ibid., p. 33.

10. Paul Tillich, "The Lost Dimension in Religion," in *Adventures of the Mind,* ed. Richard Thruelsen and John Dobler (New York: Alfred A. Knopf, 1959), pp. 50-52.

11. Tillich, "Existentialist Aspects of Modern Art," p. 141.

12. John A. Barsness, "A Question of Standard," *Film Quarterly* 21, no. 1 (Fall 1967): 33-34.

13. Robert Warshow, *The Immediate Experience* (New York: Doubleday and Co., 1962), p. 94.

14. Barsness, "A Question of Standard," pp. 36-37.

15. Stephen Farber, review of *Hombre* and *Welcome to Hard Times, Film Quarterly* 21, no. 1 (Fall 1967): 54.

16. Tillich, "Existentialist Aspects of Modern Art," p. 147.

17. Martin Esslin, *The Theatre of the Absurd* (Garden City, N.Y.: Doubleday and Co., 1961), p. 290.

18. Paul Tillich, "Protestantism and the Contemporary Style in the Visual Arts," *The Christian Scholar* 40, no. 4 (December 1957): 311.

19. Bela Balazs, *Theory of Film* (London: Dennis Dobbson, 1952).

20. Siegfried Kracauer, *Theory of Film* (New York: Oxford University Press, 1960), p. 309.

21. Haig P. Manoogian, *The Film-Maker's Art* (New York: Basic Books, 1966), p. vii.

22. John M. Culkin, "Film Study in the High School," *Catholic High School Quarterly Bulletin* 23, no. 3 (October 1965): 1.

23. G. William Jones, *Sunday Night at the Movies* (Richmond: John Knox Press, 1967), pp. 19-20.

24. Paul Tillich, *Theology of Culture* (New York: Oxford University Press, 1959), p. 49.

Carl Skrade

25. Hubert Meeker, "Blow-up," *Film Heritage* 2, no. 3 (Spring 1967): 15.

26. Harry E. Smith and Richard van Voorhis, *Ultimate Questions in Penultimate Form* (St. Louis: United Campus Christian Fellowship Publications Office, 1963), p. 2.

27. Finley Eversole, ed., *Christian Faith and the Contemporary Arts* (Nashville: Abingdon Press, 1963), p. 6, citing Bernard Scott.

# 2

# The Image of Man
# in the Recent Cinema

John C. Cooper

Every philosopher loves to talk about the weltanschauung or world view of the nation or period he is discussing. Indeed, the conception of a world outlook (or manner of interpreting the world of experience) is quite common among all educated groups in our society. Journalists and preachers, professors and novelists, write about and speak to the several world views that characterize our time. But I would like to argue that more basic to one's understanding and interpretation of the lived world in which we find ourselves than the world view we hold is our vision of man, which is the foundation for our vision of the world in general.

## The Image or Vision of Man

The concept of "the image of man" or "vision of man" that I am referring to is perhaps more theological than philosophical or anthropological. Briefly, an image of man is a basic mental picture of how a man thinks of himself and of other men. It is not the same concept as that of "the body schema," described by the psychiatrist J. Gerstmann[1] as "the inner picture or model which one forms in one's mind of one's body or one's material self, in the course of life." Rather, what I mean by an image or vision of man is what the late Paul Tillich meant by a "view of man" in his 1965 seminar on "The Christian View of Man," held at the University of Chicago. In this sense of a view of man, the basic Christian vision was one that "saw" man as having a threefold nature. This nature included the estimate that man was created good by God, created in the image of God, and that man was a complex creature formed of body and spirit. In contrast to this basic (or ancient) Christian vision, some philosophers also recognize a classical or Greek vision of man and a "modern scientific" view of man. The philosopher Harold H. Titus describes the classical view as chiefly interpreting man as a rational being. Most clearly seen in the dialogues of Plato, the Greek vision saw rationality as the highest part of the soul of man. In Aristotle's works, also, reason is the highest faculty of the human soul. "Mind is the unifying and organizing principle and, as such, is distinguished from the body. Reason is the pride and glory of man. . . . The intelligent man is the virtuous man. To know the right is to do it. Vice is the result of ignorance."[2]

In the modern scientific view of man, we meet an image that demonstrates the power of man's reason by virtue of its completeness of detail, but which downgrades man's uniqueness, regardless of his rationality. The scientific view varies from scientific discipline to discipline but agrees on certain basic points. First, man is a part of nature and is subject to physical and chemical laws just like any other organism. Again, man is seen to be one of the animals that lives on the earth. He is related to all the other living things he encounters. Most closely, he is related to the higher primates. The recent best seller *The Naked Ape*[3] made this relationship strikingly clear. At the same time, however, the physical and mental characteristics that set man apart from the other animals are recognized by the various sciences from physiology to anthropology.

*Recent Cinematic Images of Man*

When one turns from the theologians and the philosophers on the one hand, and from the physiologists and anthropologists on the other, to recent films such as *Cool Hand Luke, Blow-up, Bonnie and Clyde, The Graduate,* and *2001—A Space Odyssey,* he turns to a completely different vision of what man is. Instead of a rational creature whose glory is his mind, we meet a recent college graduate who doesn't want to do anything, particularly if it is rational to the folks over forty (*The Graduate*). Instead of a man made in the image of God, we meet a man most assuredly made in the image of a moronic fall in the direction of least resistance, with not even the sinfulness to want sexual intercourse with the girl he has "led astray" (*Bonnie and Clyde*). Instead of man, a part of nature and related to the other living creatures of the earth, we have "man the cool," separated from all other living creatures, even from his own special, living vicariously through the lens of a camera (*Blow-up*). If *The Graduate, Bonnie and Clyde,* and *Blow-up* stopped *where they started* in portraying man today, then we would have to agree with the reactionary criticisms made of each of these films, that they were dehumanizing and even sordid. But these films only begin with these surface impressions of what man actually sees himself to be in the last half of the twentieth century. All of these films go on to more human, even more spiritual, statements about what man is and about what has dehumanized and dirtied him and made him the unhappy creature he is shown—at first—to be. It is in the fully expressed statements of what man is in all three of the previously named films, plus the image of what man ought to be expressed in *Cool Hand Luke,* that we see a new and distinctly postmodern (and honest) vision of man. This vision of man communicated through these films and others like them is worthy of our attention and respect as concerned late-twentieth-century persons, and especially so if we consider ourselves religious men. I would like to attempt to systematically describe the elements that make up this new cinematic symbol of what man is and of what man ought to be.

*The Image of Man as He Is Now According to the Recent Cinema*

Man is a bundle of "matter hurrying aimlessly"—to borrow a phrase from A. N. Whitehead—according to the anthropology or vision of man conveyed by many recent films. Moreover, man is a material object who defines himself materialistically, according to

these same films. Man simply becomes aware of his own consciousness while he is already thrown, apparently aimlessly, into existence. In this state of aimlessness (and thus meaninglessness) man
sets goals for himself that are immediately gratifying and usually
sensual, indirectly if not actually directly. This material creature
is most of all competitive, or if by reason of some flaw he is not
then he is abnormally anticompetitive. Man, too, is a solitary
animal who wants freedom and release from the agonizing hurrying of matter and the conflict of competition, even if he seeks this
solitude and peace by immersing himself in other people en masse
or through attempting to dominate all others. One thing man is
not: he is not free. He is not spontaneous, for if he appears to
show such spontaneity he is immediately suspected of being queer
or odd. Every man's hand is raised (at least theoretically) against
every other, and he is in a lockstep of conformity to this social
struggle or he is not accepted. Selfishness, hedonism, cynicism are
accepted as the norms of life by men themselves, according to
these recent films, and these films show that although men define
themselves in these brutal ways they are not enough. In theological terms, the condition of sin points toward the need of grace,
and the sole apparent means of this needed grace is other people.

In *The Graduate* we are confronted with a young man who
senses the meaninglessness of his existence to the full. Ben represents the wildly anticompetitive reaction to life in the twentieth
century; his aversion to competition was so strong that he evidently refused to compete for the sexual favors of girls in his own
age group. Ben can see no point to entering the lifestream of the
upper middle class to which he obviously belongs. He is not
angry with his parents, his is simply turned off by them. His
infatuation with Mrs. Robinson is funny and pathetic at the same
time, but quite believable since she represents the line of least
resistance. Ben's sin is not fornication so much as it is sloth. The
scenes in which he floats aimlessly on a rubber mattress in his
pool drinking beer all day, dressing only to go meet Mrs. Robinson
at night, characterize the life of one who has "dropped out." Clearly
he is more naturally attracted to females of his own age since he

falls for Mrs. Robinson's daughter when the opportunity is thrust upon him. But it is interesting to note that the opportunity has to be pushed his way.

The image of man that comes across as Ben begins to take on a fuller dimensionality is that of a perverted innocent. He is neither completely evil nor for that matter completely mature. He is not without conscience; in fact, he has a very well-developed middle-class conscience since his liasion with Mrs. Robinson continues to trouble him. If there is evil in the movie, it is symbolized by the older woman, particularly in the scene where Mrs. Robinson finds Ben with her daughter, Elaine. In one of the finest moments of acting in the recent cinema, Anne Bancroft conveys to the audience a symbol of the end result of evil, death. But Ben has more than the remnants of a middle-class conscience; he is a transitional man in several respects. First, he is transitional between the over-thirty group and the teen-age group since he portrays a college graduate which would in real life make him about twenty-one, although he seems to be much older (and in fact was almost thirty when the movie was made). In the dramatic presentation he also portrays both the older moral code and the ethics of what I have called "the New Mentality."[4] It is because of his wonderfully comic portrayal of the New Mentality that *The Graduate* is such a significant motion picture. These elements include the sense of aimlessness that the younger generation feels when faced with the busy projects of the middle class, the sense of outrage at the hypocrisy of the older generation in twisting its loudly announced code to suit its own purposes (Mrs. Robinson being the chief sinner in this regard), and the rejection of the institutional emptiness of Christianity. What is so comic, both to Mrs. Robinson within the script itself and to the audience from the outside, is that Ben despises the wickedness and hypocrisy that he in fact is enjoying throughout most of the picture. And he is enjoying it in two complimentary ways—directly by sensual pleasure and indirectly by the warped pleasure of a tortured conscience. Plainly, Ben enjoys being miserable in the psychological sense while he seems to need physical comfort and sensation. In this double attraction to the luxuries of life provided by the older middle class, Dustin Hoffman as Ben is a perfect representation of the younger generation and the existentially oriented New Mentality. This younger generation, like Ben in the movie, needs and enjoys the comforts of our society and despises them at the same time. Ben—like the rebelling youth of today—recognizes that he is being "had" by the older generation, but also knows that being "had" is fun too! It wants to float on its raft with a can of beer and do nothing else. And because it senses that what it enjoys has come through injustice and out of a system it is rejecting, it, like the Buddhist who has enjoyed fresh meat, despises itself. The double enjoyment is psychological also, for the tortured conscience is the most treasured experience of what is basically a very romantic film about a very romantically inclined generation. There are few pleasures to match self-accusation and self-punishment. What some young men and women have done to themselves by living on a few hamburgers a week, going barefoot and in rags, and living in cold-water flats as hippies, Ben does in his patient wandering over the university campus looking for Elaine. And when he finds her he hurts her and he hurts himself. Not very different, perhaps, from what we older folk do to each other, but still characteristic of what is happening among young people today.

There is more to Ben's pursuit of Elaine than the simple yearning of youthful flesh for youthful flesh. As the movie makes clear, he needs her in order to complete his own soul, and she needs him. Both need to find in each other that which, the movie very preachily suggests, was not given them by their parents. From the point where the two young people decide they must have each other and the older people decide they must not have each other, the image of man presented by the film becomes *what man ought to be,* and the play becomes a comedy again. Of course, the natural aversion of Mrs. Robinson to the thought of her former lover marrying her daughter is humanly understandable. What is not understandable is the cynical marrying-off of Elaine to the medical student for the sake of appearances. And what is downright outrageous, most especially to the sensitive feelings of the New Mentality, is the hypocrisy of both sets of parents (neither of whom was morally pure) and the emptiness of the church which performed (or was about to perform) the meaningless ceremony. In one of the most cutting critiques of the church ever filmed, we see the young Ben cut off from Elaine by the church building itself—the church being represented by the glass partition against which he beat his fists. From the sanctuary the appearance of holiness serves as a backdrop for the silent curses of the adults who screamed, soundlessly, for Ben to go away. But Ben enters the church and, like a Christian crusader, snatches up the cross from the altar and swings it like a sword against his enemies. Ben and Elaine escape, and in a dropped-out, hippie fashion ride away on the bus; he in ragged dungarees and she in a torn wedding dress. Apparently, they are to live happily ever after but one wonders how that is possible. Actually the theme of the New Mentality implies no such thing, for its emphasis is upon the full realization and enjoyment of the moment, not on living happily ever after. What has been given is a new myth, a myth of the individual so honest that he or she will give up the good things given by the system for the sake of his integrity.

## 2001: The Future of Man?

The concepts of what man now is and what he ought to be is the clear theme of *2001—A Space Odyssey.* In a basic way, the film is about the nature and destiny of man. Although deeply involved in a description of man the tool-maker and his technology, the story really involves the development of the human spirit and the possibility of a transcendental leap to a new stage of evolution, the more-than-man. Just as the ground-apes were shown to have devised tools and made, thereby, the leap to man, the theme music of "Thus Spake Zarathustra" suggests that man may one day leap beyond himself to something beyond man. The question left unanswered by this film is whether this "new creature" represents a desirable advance over what man now is, as well as leaving unanswered the more basic question as to *what* this "new creature" is to be.

In impressionistically describing what man now is, or soon will be, the film, despite its fascination with space technology (and it is quite accurate, scientifically), is actually an antitechnology broadside. The struggle between man and the machine—in the shape (or the "person") of HAL 9000—is dramatically portrayed. In this struggle, man overcomes the machine, but it is a near thing. The most fascinating feature of this segment of the film to me was the fact that HAL 9000 comes across to the audience (or fellow participators) as more human than the two space travelers, Bowman and Poole. It is Hal who "sins," Hal who does evil, Hal who deceives and lies; and it is Hal who fears death as the astronaut disconnects Hal's tremendous "brain." By contrast, the human beings seem "programmed" and "preset" to complete their mission, no matter what its meaning or its costs.

The ending of the movie, with its psychedelic color-trip through space and the arrival of the ship over Jupiter, along with the arrival of the mysterious "black block," escapes rational interpretation. Obviously, from the romantic music and the mythological surroundings, man is supposed to be progressing toward that something beyond man, or "the higher man" called for by Nietzsche. But exactly what is this "higher man" to be? There is no answer given to this since the movie ends with a fetuslike shape—although a shape of things to come—floating in space like a biological question mark.

## Blow-up

*Blow-up* in one respect is as modern as tomorrow and in another as old (as McLuhan would say) as movable type. It is a film that gives us, in short, an eye for an ear. In this excellent portrayal of the human condition as it is now, we have an extension of the theme of the 1930s film *Ich Bin Ein Kamera*. The central figure of the film, a young London photographer, is "cool" to the point of an almost complete disassociation from the human hustle and bustle around him, viewing the world (and really "seeing it") only through the lens of his camera. In the terms of existentialism and phenomenology, his "intentionality" functions only through film. The young photographer shows both the fanaticism of the inspired artist and the repulsion of those badly hurt by life and other people in his response (or lack of it) to the events around him. His life lies not in the streets and parks where he walks and works, but in the darkroom and drying studio where he studies his own photographs.

The play is full of good theater, and manages to give the viewer an almost unbelievable number of fine camera shots from unusual angles, but its overarching theme is the depiction of a life of non-involvement in other peoples' lives (as in the anonymity of urban life) as a nonhuman style of life. The young man's cool "missing" of the possible murder of a fellow human being at the beginning of the movie begins to become "hot," "hotter," and "hottest" precisely through his intensive study of the photographs he made on that occasion. A really fundamental philosophical question arises when we ask ourselves whether, even in his most "hot," humanly involved period, he is not responding to the fixed ("eternal") media of his photographs or to the human being he merely "glimpsed" (and didn't "see") at the time of the suspected "murder."

Eventually, the young man evidently does come to believe that he is more than a camera, which only records events without bearing any relationship of responsibility or interest to these events, and is, indeed, a human being. Whatever else human beings may be, the picture suggests (and they may be in fact only physical organisms looking for stimulation [the orgy scene] or may simply be monkeys playing with toys [the photographer]) they are centers of responsibility who must bear the responsibility for their decisions or failures to make decisions. In fact, the last wild scenes of the make-believe tennis game and the wild auto ride suggests that the world, rather than being a series of "givens" (like tennis nets and balls, roads and rules), is actually created by the free (free from the rules of logic as well as free of custom or of physics) decisions of free human beings doing whatever

33

they will. It is an existentialist movie, in the primary sense of that term.

*Violence, Sex, and "Camp"*

The image of what man has made of himself to be has never been so crushingly—and entertainingly—displayed than in the tragicomedy *Bonnie and Clyde*. This great movie (I can honestly use no other term, for I thought it really great) presents "modern man—the mixed up" and shows us that he is like ourselves for he is one of us. As the *Time* cover story of December 8, 1967, put it: "They kill and rob banks; but they share the common concerns of common men."⁵ Bonnie is a vacant-minded, beauty-conscious, sex-oriented young girl like millions of other high school, college (and working) girls of the 1930s or 1970s. She is looking for a man with good looks who excites her and who will extricate her from the boredom of her small-town life. Bonnie's first tragedy was that she had the good looks and the excitement but not much else. Clyde wanted excitement and thrills, above all; plus the money needed for clothes, good food, liquor, and the adulation of the crowd. Part of this image of the popular, outstanding man-of-the-world is a pretty girl, and Clyde needed Bonnie to fulfill that part of the bill. Unfortunately, due to psychological complications, Clyde didn't need Bonnie for anything more personal—at least not at first. Here is a real switch in film-making, although it is a completely realistic switch; Clyde is an antihero, in the current style, but he is not as strongly sexually oriented as are most antiheroes. Clyde, then, is a truly common man; the image of what we have made ourselves in the twentieth century: demythologized, desexualized, almost dehumanized. He has *become* his porkpie hat, big revolver, and fast-moving car. We identify with him because we too have become our clothes, our "tools," our cars.

The fact that the high school dropout mindlessness and amorality of Bonnie and Clyde are lifted up as an image of our culture should not cause us to cry "foul." We must remember that they are highly intelligent ones. Bonnie and Clyde, even in the movie, almost come off as "gifted" compared with C. W. Moss and as paragons of integrity compared to the older Moss who sells them out.

The much-remarked quality of essential "innocence" in Bonnie and Clyde is a society-wide phenomenon too. Although they are capable of bestial cruelty, neither C. W., Bonnie, nor Clyde is really vicious. Rather, their cruelty is that of young children pulling the wings off butterflies. They are savage due to their ignorance. They become destructive because their unthinking actions cause them to be pushed into a corner where they must strike out. Because they possess automatic weapons their striking out is smashing, hammerlike, deadly, rather than the simple thudding of fists thrown by infantile drunks in a bar fight.

What frightens and sobers us is the overall "normality" of the Barrows gang. They are simply lower-class people, a family even, in the interlude between crimes. The social comment immediately arises that we are all like them, capable, through our ignorance and insensitivity, of utter cruelty and aimless violence. Perhaps the direction of American society with its ghetto conditions that push people into a frustrated corner where they eventually explode into fury, and its foreign policy that directs young men to places where burning villages and killing indiscriminately are "normal" acts, presents the same syndromes as Bonnie and Clyde.

But the film also contains comments on what man ought to be as well as descriptions of what man is. Bonnie and Clyde are sentimentalists, to be sure (as most people at their social level tend to be), but the feelings of family ties and loyalty to one another (and to their group) that they exhibit seem, to most of us, "good" qualities. Bonnie and Clyde are sensitive, too, although in a very lowbrow way. Bonnie writes poetry, poetry which predicts that the gang will receive the wages of sin: death. Throughout this stream of sentimentality runs a deep-seated belief in the fundamentalistic version of Christian ethics. However, it is in the love which arises not simply out of sexual attraction *but in spite of it* that Bonnie and Clyde (in the movie, if not in life) point beyond themselves toward a better way of life. Bonnie loves Clyde,

35

even with his psychological defect that so frustrates her, and in a scene at once sensual and redemptive, she liberates Clyde from the bondage of impotence. It may seem a crass thing but it is an indication of the kind of persons we might all become: healers of one another, servants of each other, unselfish men and women.

We could make too much of the overt social comment in the film. Certainly in the film and in the historical record itself, Bonnie and Clyde were folk-heroes. There was a feeling of social (lower-class) solidarity between the gang and the people of the harsh Western lands. In a single symbolic scene, Clyde gives his pistol to a dispossessed farmer who shoots holes in the homestead taken from him by an impersonal (upper-class) bank. Like Mao's and Che's guerrilla fighter, Bonnie and Clyde (up to the point where old Moss betrays them in order to save his son) swim in the water of the people and so avoid capture. It almost seems like a socialistic comment, "we against them," and yet neither the real gang nor the movie portrayal has developed this element strongly. Like the lower and lower-middle classes from which they came, Bonnie and Clyde are apolitical. They do not like the bankers and the police, but they make no ideology of their dislike. Rather than resist economic pressure directly, they prefer to avoid its power by shifting and changing: Bonnie and Clyde flee to another place; the landless farmers migrate toward California.

At the last, the suggestion as to what man ought to be in this film is only a subtle hint. And even this hint is paradoxical, like the existentialism of Jean-Paul Sartre and the lyrical tragedy of Albert Camus which inspired (or made clearer) the popular hint it offers. What Bonnie and Clyde essentially say is this: Be loyal to one another, for loyalty alone is stronger than death. And, more than loyalty alone to that one closest to you in the struggle of life, be loyal to man, especially to your own kind. Men cheat and steal and lie and kill and abandon, but we ought not to cheat or steal or lie to (although we may lie for) one another; nor ought we to kill our own kind or abandon our friends even in the face of death. And insofar as we are able we ought to share with, to love and heal, each other.

36

This is the philosophy of the *Marquis,* of the *Resistance* member (French in 1944; American in 1969), of the combat Marine, the Commando, the criminal, the drifter, the dope addict, the outcast, in short, *of the outsider.* This is the ethic of the survivor, the escaped-from-death who knows he will not always escape. And this is the image of what man ought to be in an age of violence that possesses the ultimate instruments of violence and the mindless drift that makes the use of such instruments a live possibility.

### Christ: The Careless and the Concerned

*Cool Hand Luke* remains good theater under any interpretation, but the various characteristics of the film (and its rather obvious symbolism) make it most understandable as a kind of lower-class Dostoevskian passion play in which the Christ-Idiot is not a prince but a prisoner. Luke is the twentieth century's image of the historical Christ-figure: dropped-out, an outsider, careless of the cares and interests of the material world, antipathetic to the traditional religion around him, an inspirer of senseless cruelty without being overtly evil or aggressive, but by reason of *simply being what he is.* Luke, too, is redemptive in his effects, a healer and a binder together of man, as well as a figure who receives unmerited suffering. He is human, all too human, in that he does not want to die or suffer beyond endurance. In a magnificent stroke that makes Luke an antiheroic image of Christ rather than an unbelievable (and unavoidable) hero, Luke "breaks" his suffering. Luke, moreover, is a quester for God, although a rejecter of the traditional ideas of God. Luke dares the hurler of the lightning to strike him down; Luke rejects the depthless comfort of the old-time religion of one of his guards when his mother dies. Luke ridicules, in a way frightening and disturbing to the guards and prisoners alike, the theology of the "plastic Jesus" which is endemic among fundamentalist Protestants and traditionalist Catholics. And yet, against God, Luke searches for the God-beyond-God, whom Luke finds, if at all, only in the silence of the deserted country church and in the solidarity and fellowship of those under the same sentence of life and death as he. At

37

the end, Luke is struck down with the same senseless but effective swiftness that Christ experienced as he is shot in the church window when the "man in the sunglasses" nailed him to his cross.

What is man? As a totality, Cool Hand Luke replies that man is many things. He is harsh and cruel; he is self-serving and unthinking. He is strong and weak by parts and at various times and places. He is a loner and a social creature; he is a hurter and a healer. And above all, man needs other men. "Cool Hand Luke" would not have been "Cool Hand Luke" without the fellow prisoners who responded to his "coolness" and the morale-raising power he brought, any more than Christ would have been The Christ without those who received him and his healing power as The Christ. Man is the creature who needs other men for his completion more than he needs anything material—that is the "message" of *Cool Hand Luke*.

What, then, ought man to be? Why, more like Luke, able to roll with the punches of life without becoming bitter or being "broken" in his personal center; more like Luke in being a healer and a knitter-together of human beings without becoming a dictator; more like Luke, a questioner without giving up the quest, religious without being sentimental, tough without being cruel, careless of self but not careless of others.

Finally, this movie, like *Bonnie and Clyde* in that both deal with antiheroes who stand outside the laws of man, might be given an ideological interpretation. Obviously, the men on Luke's chain gang are the impoverished and ignorant as well as the wicked. Obviously, the administration of the camp and its guards represent the power of a society more concerned with its security than with justice. (Like America today?) The film could be taken as a lower-class comment on the war of "us against them." But this sociological level is transcended—indeed it hardly comes into view—for if Luke represents, as I think he does, the ever fresh power of human love and courage and its constant creativity, then the guards that persecute and finally kill Luke represent the dark side of human beingness (much more than the peripheral violence seen in the prisoners) that incarnates evil. The "man in the sun-glasses" is the symbol of institutionalized, efficient, and self-protective violence. He is the "executioner" whom all men should resist, according to Albert Camus and our own best impulses. Beyond all accidents of space and time, race and class—like the crucifixion itself—the passion of Cool Hand Luke can be seen as the inevitable clash of good and evil, between the personalizing and the depersonalizing forces in our common *lebenswelt*.

What ought man to be? A personalizer; an individual who lives to help and heal; a resister of evil in all its forms. To paraphrase Albert Camus, whose beautiful and true description of what the gospel really is surpasses all theology, one should believe that touching one moronic convict with the feeling of human worth is more valuable than saying a thousand masses. "A new commandment I give to you, that you love one another."

## NOTES

1. *Archives of Neurology and Psychiatry* (1942), 48.
2. Harold Titus, *Living Issues in Philosophy,* 4th ed. (Cincinnati: American Book Co., 1964), pp. 143-44.
3. Desmond Morris, *The Naked Ape* (New York: McGraw-Hill Book Co., 1967).
4. John C. Cooper, *The New Mentality* (Philadelphia: Westminster Press, 1969).
5. *Time,* December 8, 1967, p. 68.

# 3

# Film, Preaching, and Meaning

Robert W. Jenson

I

The given for hermeneutical reflection is ourselves achieving or failing to achieve our lives. This task of our lives is an inescapably joint enterprise, for each new challenge or threat, each new possibility, is posed to me by some other, and I move on with my life in that he and I achieve some common understanding. The enterprise of existence is made up of multifarious occurrences of communication.

Our symposium turns attention to those events of communication in which film plays a significant role. For several generations, the experience of film has moved ever closer to the center of our self-achievement. It is, therefore, no unimportant hermeneutical question which asks: In what way or ways is the shape of the event of communication determined by the use of film?

The shape traced by a hermeneutical analysis is a temporal shape. In one way or another, every event of communication rhymes the past with the future; the present is as real as the rhyming. When we address each other, you and I are each present to the other as the one he *already* is, as the Jones or Jenson who would be identified by a biography, by a list of "the one who ..." expressions in which the blank would in each case be filled by a past-tense clause. Yet what I achieve in this confrontation is that true self who I am *not yet;* this futurity is as real to me as your

difference from me, as those marks of your life which I share
by your address to me, but share as, perhaps, your achievemen
but my mere possibility. Or put it this way: every communicatior
depends on the inheritance of language, on the entire deposit o
custom which lets me hear (*dōr*) as something to enter by. Our
address to each other depends absolutely on successful past com
munication, on how it has been done *before*. Yet when commu
nication succeeds, success is marked by the creation of *new*
language, the language of our new mutual understanding.

Every communication somehow rhymes past and future in the
present moment. The question in each case is: How this time?
Moreover, every answer to this question determines a theology
The possibility of a coherence of past and future is what is
meant by "eternity," and eternity is the defining characteristic o
the gods. Every achieving of understanding, in its particular way
of rhyming past and future, is therefore the revelation or pseudo
revelation of a particular eternity, that is, of a particular god or se
of gods. And an analysis of that way is a doctrine of the being o
that god.

## II

What goes on film is sounds and sights. We think first of the
sights and tend to consider film a visual medium; but this is ar
obvious mistake, the causes of which we will come to. Neverthe
less, we too will begin with sights. Any sort of visually apprehensi
ble shape can go on film; we will deal only with those produced by
photography or animation, with "pictures" of something. This
anyway covers more films than one would have expected ir
advance.

The function of any picture is to allow us to see what would
otherwise be absent. Between past and future, it is the present o
things that is visible; I cannot see what is no more or is not yet
The horizon of sight is space and not time. Thus a picture make
present (in the double sense of the word), or spatializes, wha

would otherwise be removed by time. Moreover, it does so in a repeatable way: if I have the picture I can at any time I will see what is in it, and this power is part of the experience even if in fact I look only once. Thus a picture establishes a present transcendent to time, and delivers this transcendence to my will. This was the ancient power of the image, which could conjure the presentness even of those made past by death (that the dead should be heard, on the other hand, has never been thought remarkable).

The present established by a picture is the presence of the past, rather than of the future. Each present moment means either the persistence of the past or an opening to the future—this is the great theological alternative. But one cannot take a picture of the future; the content of a picture when I look at it is always a part of some past state of the world. We can of course make pictures of the future as we envision it, as in science fiction films. But to do this we must simulate our vision, so that the picture delivers the future to us as if it were past—a hermeneutical point about science fiction it would be interesting to follow.

Thus the transcendent present enabled by a picture has the transcendence of stasis, of recollection. One of the main reasons for which we have traditionally assembled pictures has been to see our ancestors and important moments in our own pasts. We have wanted to assure ourselves that we are not rootless, that we now possess a past. And insofar as we have sought a similar security in our gods, we have wanted pictures of them as well. Insofar as our gods have had the eternity of timelessness, insofar as we have possessed in them the continuing reality of an *arche,* of a permanently available Beginning, we have mediated their presence by pictures. Images have been the indispensable artifacts of such mythic religion and its search for security in a changeless order.

Yahweh, the God of Israel, could have no pictures, for his transcendence was not the immutability of the past; his transcendence was the uncontrollability of the future. He was not God in that he assured Israel of stability in an Origin; he was God in that he challenged Israel to move into the unknown. The image-

43

lessness of Yahweh had nothing to do with any more spiritual conception of deity; indeed, Israel, unlike Greece, never attained any conception of other-than-material reality. You cannot make a picture of the future, Yahweh was essentially the Coming One and therefore you could not make a picture of Yahweh. A divine picture had a priori to be of some other god, and so a means of apostasy. The prohibition was verified when Yahweh raised Jesus from the dead, and so identified himself as the power of life in spite of death, of a future beyond every end.

The next step: film delivers *moving* pictures. This is the great fascination which pulled two generations into the movie palaces. Moving pictures are the very triumph of the picture, for here the picture's timeless present captures time itself. A film does not merely record one moment; it captures a history with all its temporal successiveness, its past and present and future, intact, and delivers it into space, into a disposable present. Moving pictures do in their way what Hegel did philosophically.

Moving pictures are therefore the ideal medium of a certain kind of mythic religion: the "god of our fathers" variety. In this sort of religion, God is identified not merely by one moment of the Beginning, but by a past history; he is the one who led us out of Egypt and thereby established a security which is now our right, or he is the one in whom our brave boys in their recent foxholes all trusted and were saved. The deity of this god is the timeless presence of the past history. This is the religion of Israel before the prophets revolutionized it; or it is that nationalized version of "historical religion" which has been America's civic faith. Moving pictures are the only possible images of such gods. The great sentimental biblical epics, and the religious glorifications of Americanism, were authentic and inevitable expressions of the genius of the movies, and were quite properly experienced by most in their audiences as true communications of their deepest religion.

A last step on this line: We have assumed so far that the time sequence of images on the film follows that of the history of which they are a picture, but this need not be so. The editing process perhaps the very heart of film-making, delivers the time sequence on the film to the will of the film-maker. At the same time, the pictures' reference to an actual or presumed past history in the world remains, so that the film-maker's alterations show and his lordship of the sequence of the film's time becomes itself visible. Where this possibility is taken up, the film-maker himself steps into the place of the god of past history; the present of the picture, in its transcendent inclusion even of the sequence of time, is *his* present determined in its internal order by his decision. The obvious example is *Last Year at Marienbad,* not because it was such a good film but because in it this possibility was played with so blatantly as to become unmistakable in its implications.

Within the history narrated by such a film, no god can appear. For the god communicated by such a film is the film-maker himself, and, insofar as the film lets us share his existence as our possibility, the beholder himself. The openly edited film is the ideal medium of human self-deification—as, of course, a specific sort of god, the god of a past history.

There are two forms of this deification. The film-maker's and beholder's deification may be romantic: it may mean their acquiring the traditional attributes of God. Here film functions as the supreme medium of the novel's omnipotent and omniscient author. The chief time-ruling technique is the flashback. Most fine films of the past were supernovels of this sort.

But if I am God I need only look at this slightly differently for it to have the opposite of the romantic meaning: God may acquire my attribute of finitude. This is the nihilistic move: if I am the only God, then God is nothing much. Film is perhaps the only adequate medium of one kind of nihilistic religion, the kind after historical religion, the kind which has lost faith in a god of our fathers. With arbitrary cuts and transpositions the film-maker can break the time sequence of the pictured history, in which successive events explained or meant each other. Film can do what no other visual medium can do, teach us to see the *succession* of events as meaningless, as temporally disconnected and arbitrary. It is this kind of nihilism which is ours (rather than any genuinely

Buddhistic variety) and which is the point of most currently haile‹ films.

Therefore film, in its romantic/nihilistic ambivalence, is ou‹ specific medium. Perhaps no other way of communication is ad‹ quate to the word of late-twentieth-century America's god, th‹ god of a faith which inherently fluctuates between the most arr‹ gant religiosity and a uniquely comprehensive denial. It is n‹ accident that the present generation of students, more transpar‹ ently and narrowly American than any before it, finds films th‹ only literature that does not drag; and that where students i‹ other countries are most Americanized (if largely by anti Americanism) the same taste appears. There is a specific spiri‹ tuality which can express itself in words only as "like mayb‹ Zen—but not really." It is often intensely religious, but know‹ a god only in the endlessly reiterated rejection of any god of it‹ fathers. This spirituality is foreordained for film. Or, rather, i‹ would have been impossible without film.

## III

We must already raise the question of the possible role of fil‹ in the communication by which *Christian* faith lives. The herme‹ neutic character of film is such that filmed communication is eac‹ time the revelation of a mythic god, and, in the full developmen‹ of film's special possibilities, of the special mythic god of late twentieth-century America. That is, film is the unique medium o‹ our particular "natural" faith.

Therefore, one's estimate of film's possibilities for Christia‹ communication will depend on how he settles the whole issue o‹ the relation of the gospel to the word of a natural faith. This is ‹ matter much too large to argue here; I will merely state som‹ alternatives. If one holds that grace always perfects nature an‹ never attacks it, he will simply set out to make films with Chri‹ tian narrative content. If one holds that some "natural" faiths ar‹ suitable preparations for Christian faith, while others are not, h‹

will probably find this romantic/nihilistic natural religion unsuitable and polemicize against "modern" movies. If one suspects a radical dichotomy of nature and grace, he may reject film altogether as a medium of the believing word. I myself think that the word of the gospel is always addressed to man in the language of his natural faith, yet is polemic against that faith. The gospel is always a communication which occurs in the course of our natural religious quest, yet is directed against it. It should, I think, be possible for a film to use its hermeneutic possibilities polemically against the very religion they intrinsically posit. For this to be so, however, there must be more to say about film's hermeneutic power than we have so far said. To find that more, we turn from filmed sights to filmed sounds.

## IV

Any sort of sounds can be recorded on film; we will discuss words only. As pictures present past images, so recording presents words uttered or presumed uttered in the past; and as film presents past images in their sequence as history, so film records discourse and not merely single utterances. We are not, however, so impressed with this achievement, for it is one which memory and our ability to emit sound have always enabled us to do by ourselves. Even the technological perfecting of the ability to reproduce past discourse lies far in the past, with the invention of writing. A recording, of course, brings not only the semantic substance of past utterances into the present—as writing does—but their pure sound as well. But the pure sensuality of words is the aspect in which they are most like sights, and we can deal with this aspect by simply taking our previous discussion as repeated. Anyway, the mimic capacities of the human voice anticipated also the sensual reproduction of discourse.

But although the recording of discourse is not as shocking as the reproduction of sequential images, it is an equally integral part of film, and when we take it into account it alters our hermeneutical description. At a first level, the addition of recording greatly augments the same hermeneutic powers we have already attributed to filmed images. It is by words that successive events in time mean each other, so as to cohere into history. A silently filmed sequence of images is able to capture a history only insofar as some visible shapes function like words, as certain gestures, costumes, etc., have acquired conventional semantic force. Therefore the storytelling of silent film may be powerful—in the hands of genius, more powerful than that of sound film—but has a range limited by the narrow vocabulary of such language. The addition of verbal language indefinitely expands that range.

Moreover, the sequence of words is like the sequence of images in being at the will of the editor. He can break or transpose both the given internal sequence of the recorded utterances, and their given synchronization with accompanying images. With both images and discourse on his film, the film-maker has inexhaustible subtleties of nihilistic interpretation available. The filmed event cannot merely be seen to have no meaning; it can be given an unsuitable meaning, or the meaning of some other event altogether. With words, film's nihilism can become ironic, casuistic and persistent.

So far, filmed words add nothing qualitatively new to the hermeneutic power of filmed images. But there is a way in which the film-maker can use words which radically transforms the hermeneutic situation; for words can be the present not only of the past—as can images—but also of the future. Indeed, this is their role in human life and the reason that language is essential to human being. With a word, we evoke, pray for, and above all promise what is not but—by that word—shall be. Words are the fluid of that self-projection into a future which is the substance of human life. Therefore filmed words can break the self-sufficient present of the film and its captured past, by giving that present a meaning in the life of the beholder future to the moment of beholding. An example is the dialogue between the woman and the boy in the closing moments of *The Silence*. Where this possibility is taken up, the total film can function as an affirmative word of meaning-granting address, but now one which has taken into itself and transcended the romantic/nihilistic interpretation posited by the filmed images. At the extreme limit of its hermeneutic possibilities, film can be the communication of a meaning beyond nihilism, of a hope beyond hopelessness.

## V

We merely change the idiom of the last sentence if we say: At the extreme of its hermeneutic possibilities, film could be the word of a god beyond the god of past history, even in his guise of Nothingness. There could be a communication by film the temporal shape of which identified God as a Transcendence which occurs precisely as the cancellation of the eternity of the past, as the breaking of the present moment's self-enclosure, as the grant of freedom.

Such a god would surely be the one called Yahweh, of whom the gospel speaks. It should, therefore, be possible for a film to be a sermon, and if so then precisely *the* sermon for us who achieve our lives by romantic/nihilistic interpretation of reality. In such a sermon-film, the word which broke the timeless picture-present would be some part or form of the narrative about Jesus. I suspect that such a film is still beyond us. But surely there could be and perhaps are films whose words, so to speak, leave a hole in the permanently available romantic/nihilistic present created by the film. For such a hole the Christian story would be, contingently, the only fit. Such films would be at once ultimate communications of late-twentieth-century American spirituality, and powerful indirect occurrences of the gospel (that it works out so is connected with the role of the gospel in the history which has led us to our nihilistic historicism—another topic not to be pursued here).

# 4

# Biblical Spectaculars
# and Secular Man

James M. Wall

One of my favorite Methodist bishops recently complained that he is tired of all those theologians who purport to describe secular man. "In theology," the bishop wrote, "some fellow constantly comes along to say that nobody believes this or everybody presumes that. I read this stuff and I say to myself that I do not believe it. I do not presume it, and nobody I know takes that attitude."

Since a man's view of the world is quite subjective, it is difficult to argue against such logic, i.e., I know no one like that, therefore he doesn't exist. But I would suggest that the bishop take note of the success of the 1926 silent movie *King of Kings* in comparison to the financial flop of the 1965 biblical extravaganza, *The Greatest Story Every Told.* The difference between the earlier Cecil B. DeMille film and the $18 million disaster made by George Stevens is the difference between a pseudoreligious public and today's secular public.

The secular man those "theologians" are describing is to be found staying away in droves from *Story,* the most carefully made, well-intentioned biblical film ever produced in this country. That same secular man is flocking to see such nonbiblical films as *Who's Afraid of Virginia Woolf?* and *Blow-up.* Obviously, one's case for secular man cannot rest entirely upon what films he attends. But one suspects that George Stevens will be reluctant ever again to count on a "religious" public to attend a biblical extravaganza. Indeed, *The Greatest Story Ever Told* may well be the last overtly religious film made for a mass commercial market.

It should be pointed out that the term "secular man," as I am using it, is not in opposition to "Christian" or to "churchman." The end of the biblical spectacular suggests that the basic mood of Western civilization is secular, and that the churchman, as well as the nonchurchman, shares this outlook, often to his dismay and chagrin. For example, many movie-goers (especially those church-men over forty-five) still feel that the biblical stories have the power to evoke a religious response. No doubt this is true for many of these people, even though it may be argued that much of the response to the straight, uninterpreted first-century biblical material is as much nostalgia for the religion of our fathers as it is a genuine reaction to the Jesus story. In any event, the secular man I am describing is the man who has carefully absented himself from such films as *The Greatest Story Ever Told,* even though what I shall later describe as "religious" films may have con-siderable meaning for him. I am not proposing the rejection of the biblical story, but rather that it be recognized that it may no longer be assumed ipso facto as the possessor of a power which emerges immediately upon presentation of its facts. I doubt, to be brief, the stories of those foreign nationals who picked up the New Testament tabula rasa and were immediately converted to Christianity.

Secular man, therefore, has no interest in the biblical spectacu-lar because he does not possess the basic religious presuppositions that operated within the American public prior to World War II. In *The Greatest Story Ever Told* the character of Jesus is an ethereal figure, obviously meant to be "divine," taking one look at total strangers and having them drop everything and immediately follow him down the road. For secular man, such a Jesus figure is not believable. He wants his divinity concrete and inherent within the human situation. This helps explain the mixed reaction to Pier Pablo Pasolini's *The Gospel According to St. Matthew.*

As a picture about a fiery young first-century revolutionary—sort of a young Fidel Castro—*Matthew* was superb film-making. But in those literal moments when Pasolini had his Jesus walk on water or ascend into the clouds he lost momentum and fell back to the level of a "beards-and-bathrobe" Bible film.

Broadly speaking, there are two ways a film can be made. It can be discursive and talk *about* a subject, or it can *present* its material and permit its subject matter to evolve inherently out of the material at hand. The discursive film *re-presents* material that is informational or instructive, while the presentational film utilizes its meduim to share the film-maker's vision with an audience. In the discursive film there must be either a considerable body of presupposed common material, or else the film-maker will have to spell out his presuppositions so that his information may then be imparted to his audience. The presentational film presents its theme implicitly within its materials and assumes a common humanity which transcends the varied sets of information belonging to diverse audiences. Again, broadly speaking, a presentational film could be said to exist on a continuum between a work of art and a purely manufactured formula product. To the extent that the film presents its material within the images, situations, and context of the film, it moves toward the art end of the continuum.

The biblical spectacular initially was successful because it was a discursive film which talked about a subject of common knowledge to most in its audience. Nothing within the context of *The Greatest Story Ever Told,* for example, prepares the audience for the immediate success Jesus had in assembling disciples. An earlier pietistic, or more "religious," audience assumes this success and does not have to be prepared for it within the framework of the work it is viewing. But suppose for a moment that an individual who is not familiar with the Jesus story is viewing this film. He will be puzzled by the consternation this figure causes among the crowds, and certainly—if he possesses any sense of public responsibility—he will be sympathetic to Herod and Pilate who must finally eradicate a local troublemaker. In *Story* the strongest figures are those who are upset by Jesus. Director George Stevens worked more effectively with Jesus' enemies because they displayed human emotions. Jesus was so ethereal and above the common squabbles that beset us all that he was neither believable nor attractive. His disciples were presented as mere puppets who blindly followed a man for reasons not apparent either visually or verbally. Only a biblically oriented viewer sees the reasons for their decision. These reasons are not encompassed within the framework of the film itself.

Stevens' film presupposed this knowledge and thus showed a failure to realize that while the public possesses limited information about the original first-century story it is no longer moved by it.

The biblical spectacular, therefore, is understood best as a discursive film which serves as an audio-visual aid but not as a work of art. An audio-visual aid imparts information, but it does not convince or convict an audience. Art, on the other hand, is interested only incidentally in information, and, by its very nature, is desirous of sharing a vision of life which must be accepted or rejected by its viewer.

Discursive films have their raison d'être. Children learn how corn grows through cleverly drawn sequences in a color motion picture. Companies provide information on sales techniques to their personnel by the use of an audio-visual aid film. But these are films that presuppose a desire to learn on the part of the audience; they presuppose also a certain validity of the subject matter at hand.

The biblical spectacular was a discursive film which historically, from *King of Kings,* through the *Ten Commandments, David and Bathsheba,* down to *Greatest Story,* has imparted information on Bible stories to an audience it assumed already was respectful and predisposed to accept the film's message. Through the years, as the pious public began to disappear, these biblical spectaculars jazzed up their subject matter to the point where myth, legend, and historical events blurred. The biblically illiterate "religious" public accepted this, partly because most producers learned from Cecil B. DeMille that even in religious America Bible stories sold best when garnished with sex and spice. It remained for George Stevens to exercise restraint and omit any exploitative sexual material from *Story*. This omission, plus the total secularity of the American public, guaranteed its failure.

Does the demise, however, of the biblical spectacular mean that "religion" and the secular film have parted company forever? Not at all, for the irony of Stevens' finale to the long line of biblical films is that in the very year that his film failed to receive any awards from national church groups those same groups were honoring such pictures as *The Pawnbroker* and *Nothing But a Man,* two modest-budget films which focused on a common theme of the inhumanity of man to man coupled with the indomitable spirit that permits man to achieve personal victory in the face of degradation and despair.

*Nothing But a Man,* to cite one example, is a simple tale of an Alabama Negro badly handicapped by inadequate education and a century of racial oppression. Such a subject could have been dealt with discursively. Treated in this manner, the film would have run the risk of becoming mere propaganda—the Negro's mistreatment could have been caricatured in the darkest of tones and his adversaries depicted as archvillains. But this melodramatic approach to film-making, while it may possess propaganda value, is not art, for it does not attempt to view with honesty the totality of the existential moment. The director chose, instead, to share a vision of what it means to be under oppression. The hero was portrayed with a believable ambiguity, so that when the film ended with a testament to man's will to live and love, the audience was called into a decision regarding its own desire to live and love. To see this film merely as one dealing with racial tension is to miss the deeper dimension of the celebration of humanity that is depicted.

Thus, in this time of the death of the biblical spectacular, the religious film is that motion picture which manages, through artistic utilization of its medium, to celebrate what it means to be human. In doing so, the film-maker who would locate his effort nearer the end of the continuum we have designated as art is the film-maker who works somewhere within the definition of art that Stephenson and Debrix provide in their book *The Cinema as Art*. They define art as a "process in which the artist makes use of his experience, intuition, or inspiration, selecting and arranging it to create beautiful and true artistic objects which to a greater or lesser extent imitate 'reality' . . . and that through these objects he communicated his experience to an audience."[1]

To the extent that a film is able to share a fresh vision with its audience, that vision can be said to be "religious" in the Christian sense if it celebrates humanity or if it exercises with conviction a strong agony over moments where humanity is actually distorted. *The Pawnbroker* is a film which falls in the latter category. Set in the middle of a seething Harlem, this picture presents (but does not describe, as a discursive film might do) the "deadness" of a Jewish pawnbroker whose concentration camp experiences have killed his openness toward his fellowmen. Visitors to his little shop are searching for some human contact, but the pawnbroker rejects them all. This is religious art in that the scenes which depict the distortion of humanity do so with an agonizing appropriate to those who love man. The Christian may speak of such love out of his experience in the Christian community. This does not mean, however, that the film-maker is explicitly expressing a Christian concern or that he necessarily speaks out of a Christian conviction. It does mean that the vision of humanity which he shares through his medium is a vision that the Christian can embrace as consistent with and evocative of his own vision of man. The Christian can attest that, regardless of its content, a film that is explicitly secular may possess the power to call the Christian back into a deeper and renewed awareness of his own selfhood.

It is unrealistic, of course, to assume that a commercially produced motion picture represents the vision of a single individual. Rarely does this occur, even when a film is under the exclusive control of such film directors as Sweden's Ingmar Bergman, or possibly Otto Preminger in this country. A film must be written, acted, photographed, edited, and then distributed. Considerable money is involved in each film. The average low-cost U.S. picture, for example, usually costs about one million dollars, and it is not unusual for such a film as *Who's Afraid of Virginia Woolf?* to cost $6 million (thanks in large measure to its famous stars). To compare such a complex commercial operation with an individual Van Gogh painting is to be sadly out of touch with harsh economic realities.

But even when a film is produced largely under one man's direction, that man knows that his product will not be sold to a single art-fancier. Instead, he knows a million-dollar investment must interest millions of ticket-buyers in a mass world culture. One could therefore argue that film directors such as Michelangelo Antonioni and Roman Polanski made films with greater honesty and religious potential when they lost money than now, after tasting the joys of box-office success. This conflict between commerce and art will not be resolved so long as the motion picture is a product that must be sold to large numbers in the mass public. But given these economic realities, the Christian who looks for that which he considers "religion" in a commercial film does have the single finished product to evaluate and experience. And that finished product, be it the work of one man or many, is to be considered religious to the extent that it speaks to the human situation with the authenticity shared by the individual appraising his own religious understanding of life.

Celebration of what it means to be human, of course, is a generality which can only be spelled out concretely when a particular film is under consideration. The secular Christian examines an explicitly secular film for religious content based upon his own self-conscious understanding of what it means to be a man. He must not, however, demand that the secular film-maker utilize religious symbols or forms that are unique to his particular religious understanding. The frustration that many in the older religious generation feel regarding the secular film is that it does not make religious noises that are familiar, or work within the framework of religious structures that are comfortable. *Virginia Woolf* drew upon language and situations which are largely incom-

patible with conventional Christianity. One could react to this pro-
fanity and adultery by saying, "Yes, that's the way some people
live, and we need to be aware of such people so that we can love
and understand them." I have heard pastors say they have met
George and Martha through their pastoral counseling and don't
need to see them again in a film. This is a gross misunderstanding
of this particular film; the misunderstanding comes because the
religious man is looking at *Virginia Woolf* as a discursive film
which he thinks is telling him something psychologically valid
about a fragmented marriage, or pehaps sociologically about what
goes on within college faculty families.

But *Virginia Woolf* is not a discursive film about marriage.
It is a presentational film that presents the viewer to himself
through the experience of the film. George and Martha are
Everyman, and their love-hate relationship is, to some degree,
every marriage. The task of the viewer who sees this film is to
receive or reject its vision of humanity.

*Virginia Woolf,* therefore, is not an audio-visual film on how to
conduct a party. It is a presentational "religious" film because it
celebrates humanity in a manner compatible with the understanding of that humanity which I possess because of my location within
the historic Christian community. This is the community which
looks to the Christ-event as its constitutive moment. But looking
to that moment does not mean forcibly placing it over the secular
motion picture experience to see where and if certain symbols are
*re*-presented consistent with the biblical reality. It is unwise to
watch for arms outstretched in a film and insist that the crucifixion
is here presented (as I heard one churchman do after viewing
*Rocco and His Brothers*). Or, again, in *Knife in the Water*, the
young man who brings a married couple to a point of decision
certainly performs a catalytic role in their lives, but our experience
of this film is diluted if we are too eager to seize upon the fact
that the boy races across the top of the water, lies down with
arms outstretched and a coil of rope over his head, or injures
the palm of his hand. The intention of the film artist may or may
not have been deliberately to suggest a parallel to the Christ-event,

although the parallel here has a stronger case than in most films. But to look for religious meaning through the repetition of familiar symbols is to enter the film experience with a closed attitude, thereby hampering the possibility of self-awareness which a work of art can potentially present to us.

If the Christian story with its symbols is not to be used for proof-texting a secular film, what then is the value of this story in seeking the implicit religious significance in a film? What is unique about the Christian's approach to a film if he is to consider it under the same ground rules as the non-Christian?

The answer, I think, lies in understanding that all of us approach potentially renewing cinematic experiences with a particular background and history. Our sex, age, circumstances, ability to understand film language—all contribute to that experience. The Christian, to one degree or another, approaches all experiences out of a particular history he shares with other Christians. This history varies in many ways, but there remains one constitutive point in that history, the Christ-event: the historical moment recorded in the New Testament having to do with the life, death, and resurrection of Jesus, the Christ.

Whatever that event means to the secular man who self-consciously declares himself a Christian, it will in some way affect his view of what it means to be human. It is obvious that the vision of humanity shared by the artists of our contemporary civilization has about it a certain commonality regarding what it means to be a respecter of persons, the dignity of man, the beauty of human relationships, and the loyalty to a cause, to name only a few. In this way, our common Christian history has already become the hidden agenda of modern society.

The film artist, therefore, is that man who will share his vision of life with us through his medium, and seek our response to his vision. We may reject it as superficial, inane, banal, repulsive, or merely dishonestly exploitative. We may receive the vision of the film artist as a proper celebration of what it means to possess or lose that precious commodity we know as life. The hanging scene in the short *Occurrence at Owl Creek Bridge* is such a celebration, even though the life to which we become intensely related is snuffed out. This is a film which calls upon the viewer to grasp life as something vital and meaningful, without attempting in the limits of its assigned task to spell out just how life should be lived.

Secular man, therefore, is the man who looks for the meaning of life within the framework of his own lived existence. He will no longer respond to an audio-visual statement about a first-century "divine" man. He will, however, be open to the evocative power of a film which celebrated humanity, and thereby calls us all to receive the gift of life. His openness, I submit, is further indication that secular man is deeply religious, so long as he is permitted to define his religion in terms of meaningful living.

## NOTES

1. Ralph Stephenson and J. R. Debrix, *The Cinema as Art* (Baltimore: Penguin Books, 1966), p. 17.

# 5

# Bergman and Polanski on the Death of God

William Hamilton

Yesterday's piety used to declare that the final test of a living theology lay in its being able to feed the life of prayer. Since the death of God theology must necessarily fail that test, it may as well propose another test (and, needless to say, one it can pass). So: tomorrow's piety may suggest that a theology's viability rests in whether it can be rendered visually in the medium of film. "The medium is the kerygma," you might say. Even more, it might even be suggested that the death of God theology is working these days precisely because it is the sort of theological vision that can be filmed. Can anyone really imagine a neo-orthodox movie?

The death of God means and does a number of things to artists, and that variety can be interestingly tested by examining here two quite separate film expressions of the death of God, Ingmar Bergman's trilogy: *Through a Glass Darkly, Winter Light,* and *The Silence;* and Roman Polanski's *Rosemary's Baby.*

Bergman, for the most part, is the author of his own scripts, so it is quite appropriate to speak of the films as his work. He is not a political writer, not "engaged" in the existentialist sense, and not so much dominated by twentieth-century questions. He has some-thing of the neutrality of his native Sweden, a land in which Protestantism has rather fully lost its power to persuade but in which there are still vestiges of Protestant middle-class values. It is possible to find these vestiges in Bergman himself, in his longing for some kind of moral stability, for God, for a strong family structure. More psychological than political, more Buber than Marx, Bergman seems most interested in those human problems that remain after a welfare state has achieved tolerable solutions to the questions of justice and equality.

Over this whole trilogy lies an atmosphere of threat and defeat. *Through a Glass Darkly* portrays a few isolated people on an island cut off from everything. The mood of *Winter Light* is cold and lonely, while in *The Silence* the leading characters are in a foreign land, in a deserted hotel, unable to communicate with each other or with anyone else. Unlike some of Bergman's earlier films, these three are quite free of symbolism, free even of those necessary images that distinguish a film from a sermon or a tract. He is playing the ascetic here, peeling away everything that might be considered ornament. What is he intending to say to us?

### Through a Glass Darkly

The biblical title should be noted, and the context of the phrase in Paul's meditation on love. We should note also the distinction, in 1 Corinthians 13, between the inadequate seeing we now have and the full knowledge that is promised. Thus we should not be surprised to discover that this film is about love, about some inadequate present forms of it, and about the promise of something better in the future.

The action takes place at a summer house on an island in the Baltic Sea over a twenty-four-hour period. The characters are Karin, a girl recently discharged from a mental hospital where, we discover, she had been treated for schizophrenia; her husband, a good and somewhat helpless doctor (when they are in bed that night Karin says to him, "You always do the right thing, and it is never any good"); her father, a troubled and fashionable novelist; and her adolescent brother.

The film has two themes, and it may be that they are never quite brought together. It is partly about the novelist, his fears, his failures, his remorse at his inability to love. He is caught in a crisis of sorts, a middle-age crisis of morale, and no one offers to help. At the beginning of the film, after supper, he leaves the table to look for his tobacco in his room and there he breaks down, weeping, with his body stretched in the form of a cross. He knows his own lovelessness, he is honest with himself, and we cannot but sympathize. But he is also portrayed as cold, more interested in work than his family, even willing to use his daughter's illness as material for his new novel. Bergman leaves us ambivalent about the loveless father, but he returns to the same problem again in the character of the pastor in *Winter Light.*

The second theme has to do with Karin and her mental deterioration. This deterioration is accentuated by her accidental discovery that both her father and her husband know her case to be hopeless, and it is symbolized by an incestuous attack on her brother.

The opening half-hour of this film shows Bergman at his best, portraying the deep tensions and yet well-meaning affection binding this family together. After their picnic supper, Karin and her brother put on an original play about how a poet (the father?) promises and then breaks his promise to love a princess forever. This play may be a rather clumsy attempt to offer a causal explanation for Karin's mental condition.

The next morning, the men leave the island and the brother and sister are left alone. She becomes distracted, growing more and more sensitive to sights and sounds. She finally hides in the wreck of an old ship on the shore, and in her growing fear commits incest with her young brother.

The father and husband return to the island, observe Karin's deterioration, and summon the helicopter-ambulance from the mainland. Karin has been visiting a mysterious upstairs room several times during the day, and in this room she awaits the ambulance. (The working title for this film was "The Wallpaper" and this refers to the bizarre and patterned paper on the walls of this room.) Just as we see the helicopter flash by the window of this room, from top to bottom, as it lands, spiderlike, a sort of deus ex machina, Karin receives a visitation from God in her upper room, and her God turns out to be a spider who sexually attacks her. She becomes hysterical, and after being tranquilized, she describes her vision:

> He came to me and I saw his face. It was a loathsome evil face. And he climbed up on me and tried to penetrate me. But I warded him off. And all the time I saw his eyes. They were cold and calm. When he could not enter into me he quickly climbed up on my breast and my face and then on to the wall. . . . I have seen God.

What does this all mean? Who is this "God" she has seen? Is "God" the name for her madness? Can one see God only when one is mad? Is faith the same as foolishness or madness? Schizophrenia, we know, is the inability to distinguish between the self and the world. Is this the true breakdown of the subject-object relation, the mystical oneness that men have sought?

This climax of the Karin theme is beautifully carried off in the film, and it is Bergman at his haunting best. In contrast, the final few minutes of the film are a terrible letdown. After Karin is taken away, no doubt permanently, to the hospital, Bergman turns to the theme of the father, and to his inability to love. The father is so shaken by Karin's breakdown that he is at last able to break through to his son with a true message, the message that God is love. This really doesn't convince us, for we want to know how the father found this out. Nobody loved anybody else very effectively in the film; all the human love we saw was either ineffectual or destructive. So there really isn't any preparation for the final sermon which, without preparation, becomes just a banal triviality.

Are we really meant at the end to see the father redeemed by tragedy from the prison of his lovelessness? Has Karin's death-madness, and resurrection in the helicopter, really started not only a psychological but a theological process in the loveless father? According to one published statement, it appears that Bergman wants us to see something theological going on here. It is reported that he remarked that this film, along with *Wild Strawberries* and *The Virgin Spring*, is about atonement and the problem of God.

Did he mean it? In any case, at the close of the film, the Karin theme (the relation of madness and God) and the father theme ("Daddy spoke to me" and God is love) are not brought together in a satisfactory way. Dwight MacDonald has an interesting comment on Bergman's theological interpretation of his own work:

These problems are in general meaningless to me. I don't feel guilty, I don't believe in God and am not much interested in whether I'm right or not. They sometimes become meaningful when someone like Dorothy Day, in her life, or T. S. Eliot, in his poetry, fills them with a personal, and so an original and interesting, content. This Mr. Bergman has never been able to do for me. "God is love" indeed. I was told that at compulsory chapel in Phillips Exeter Academy. What does it *mean,* exactly? When Mr. Bergman can be explicit, in cinematic terms, I shall take his Message seriously. Meanwhile, I shall continue to enjoy the secular portions of his movies.[1]

You may feel, as I do, that MacDonald is a bit shrill here, not quite relaxed enough to be wholly convincing. But the ending of *Through a Glass Darkly* is weak, not because it is theological, but because Bergman has not brought the two themes of the plot together—God as a spider and God as love. (Unless we are supposed to conclude that the final message is that God is a loving spider.)

### Winter Light

There are some obvious connections between the first and second films of this trilogy. God the spider and God as love appear in the second as well as the first. Gunnar Björnstrand plays the novelist in spiritual trouble in the first film, and the pastor in spiritual trouble in the second.

The Swedish title of *Winter Light* is literally translated as "The Communicants," meaning both the literal communicants at the sacrament at the beginning and the end of the film, and those in general who are trying to communicate to one another—and fail.

In many ways this is a better and clearer film. There is a "faultless and almost intolerable harmony here between the major theme—God is silent—and the environment" which is itself silent and noncommunicative. And the religious substance is in certain ways different. In *Through a Glass Darkly,* God is not dead or silent or absent. He is love for the father and son, and a sexually aggressive spider for Karin as she goes mad. In *Winter Light* he has disappeared. The atmosphere is doom-laden and deathly. The action takes place on a cold Sunday between the morning and evening services, and the subject is a man's crisis of faith: "How, what, whether to believe," as Stanley Kauffmann puts it. The answer: "You can't believe anything." You can talk to neither God nor man. *Through a Glass Darkly* seemed at the end to suggest that love was a way to God; at least, that if God was inaccessible the other person was not. Hence the young boy's cry of delight: "Daddy spoke to me." All this has gone in *Winter Light.* "There is no divine society, no human community; only isolated individuals and dead worship services. Bergman seems to be saying that if life was once lived in expectation of answers, it is now lived in a continuity of questions. Crisis no longer leads to resolution. For him the special agony is the tearing of the bond between God and man. Unlike Antonioni, whose work also concentrates on this matter, he does not believe that man invented God and must be manly enough to admit it and to destroy Him. Bergman is concerned to find a way of living with—at the very least—the memory of God."[2]

This is interesting, however accurate it may be as a comparison of the work of two great directors. It suggests that there are two kinds of reaction to the experience of the death of God. They can go together and they can be found separately. In one mode, man feels free and strong and takes full responsibility for his own life, his own actions, his own world. In the other, there is a pathos, a sense of loss or a memory, and there is a need to keep the space that has been vacated intact, to remember it. *Winter Light* is about the death of God in the second sense, while *Through a Glass Darkly* is not yet at that point. It still lives in the world of anguished, existential, and conventional Protestantism: God is the suffering enemy; only the fool can see him.

In any case, the action of *Winter Light* is easily described. We open on a painful service of Communion with a congregation of nine. After the service, the pastor is asked by a distracted wife to comfort her husband, a fisherman suffering from suicidal melancholy based on fear of nuclear destruction. (This is one of the rare concessions Bergman makes to the twentieth century.) Depressed by a cold, the pastor asks the fisherman to return for a talk later in the day. The pastor becomes afflicted by his own impotence, and when the fisherman does return he embarrasses the poor man by a recital of his own theological woes.

The fisherman leaves, hardly reassured, and the pastor's mistress, the local schoolteacher, presses him for marriage. The man confesses he can love no one but the memory of his dead wife. She gives him a long letter which he reads after she has left. In the scene depicting his reading of this letter, Bergman has a long close-up, a beautiful scene, and one of the few places in this film where our emotions are fully engaged. After a brutal scene in which the pastor decisively rejects the teacher's love, word comes that the fisherman has shot himself. The pastor and the teacher go to view the body, curiously unmoved, and the pastor ineptly informs the fisherman's wife. Then together they make their way to a nearby village for the evening service, where there turns out to be but one "communicant," the teacher herself, apart from the organist and the sexton.

On the way to the second service there is a fascinating touch. The pastor is speaking to his mistress about his desire to become a minister and how he had made the decision largely to please his parents. He continues to describe his call, but a passing train makes whatever he does say inaudible to us, as if such words on such a subject are rarely worth speaking or worth hearing anymore.

Just before the second service, the crippled sexton questions the pastor about the crucifixion and especially about the relation of Jesus' physical suffering to his spiritual sense of desolation. He wonders if his inability to convince the disciples and his own acute sense of God's withdrawal wasn't worse than the actual pain. This is a striking and mysterious scene. Is the sexton perhaps the devil tempting the pastor, as he tempts most of us, to confuse himself with Jesus and his suffering? So the pastor, succumbing to the temptation, accepts his suffering as participation in that of Jesus, and goes forward to conduct the service for one, godless, just like Jesus on the cross.

This is not a difficult picture to interpret or understand, for it is free of the symbolic touches Bergman liked to use in his earlier work. But some questions and problems remain to haunt us. Is the pastor supposed to achieve a true self-understanding at the end? Is his decision to continue the second service, with but one communicant, the rejected mistress, an act of heroism, a moment of "communion" (perhaps even an affirmation of the objective character of the priesthood, valid apart from man's feelings)?

The pastor has apparently become a minister, like so many unhappy men before him and since, out of consideration for his parents. He had longed for a God who would give him security, but now, it seems, he has no God and no security. Perhaps it doesn't matter to Bergman whether one has a God or not, as long as one tries to communicate, to be "a communicant." One really doubts that the pastor and his mistress will manage to speak either to God or to each other. (It should be noted, since we have been forced to see connections between the first and second members of this trilogy, that the third film is called *The Silence* and has as its main theme our friend, the problem of noncommunication.)

Do you feel, as I do, that the pastor's loss of God doesn't move us, the way a really good loss of God should? Why is this? Is it Bergman's intention, or is there something inherent in Bergman's conception of the loss or the death of God that is antiemotional and therefore unmoving? The fisherman's despair and the teacher's hopeless love, less important in the film as a whole, are far more moving. Perhaps related to this is the fact that the suicide of the fisherman affects the pastor and teacher so little. How calmly the pastor contemplates the dead man's body.

What is the correct description of the pastor's relation to God? Is God absent, dead, momentarily withdrawn? What is the role of the love of God in this film, as compared to *Through a Glass Darkly*? There we had both God and love and some attempt, rather unclear, to unite the two. Here we clearly have a permanent withdrawal of God from everyone and everything except the words of the prayer book, and an equally permanent withdrawal of love, except for the helpless, rejected love of the teacher.

### The Silence

In *The Silence* one is tempted to say that Bergman's concern about the silence of God has disappeared and that what is left is only the problem of human communication. Yet, in the printed Swedish version of the script Bergman has referred to the theme of the film as "the silence of God." We do hear, in the beginning, that the father of the two sisters, a commanding figure of authority, has died. Are we to make something of that?

Again in this film Bergman has matched his physical setting to his theme with great skill. Two sisters, Anna and Ester, are on their way to Sweden and have stopped in an unidentified foreign country, mainly because of Ester's illness. They are staying in a virtually deserted hotel. The city's location is unspecified, and the sisters cannot speak the language. The name of the city is Timoka or Timokas (related to the dative form of the Estonian word for "executioner"). We get the impression that it is somewhere in central Europe, either just before or just after a war; the two sisters and the child seem to be refugees.

On their arrival at the hotel, Ester, the intellectual, takes to her bed. Anna is the sensual sister, restless and bored. We sense at once an unexplained hostility between the sisters and perhaps even a trace of a former or present lesbian relationship between them.

The contrast between the two sisters is sharply drawn from the start: Anna enjoying her own body and that of her son in a natural, almost pagan, way; Ester, the bored intellectual, ill and alone. The portrait of Ester's loneliness is brilliant: the cigarette put out in the overflowing ashtray, her wandering nervously about the room, looking out the window, ringing for a bottle, falling back on the bed, all this coming to a climax in the astonishing masturbation scene. This whole scene, so beautifully portrayed by Ingrid Thulin, is an example of how Bergman builds a character by piling one particular observation on another.

Anna is just as bored and restless, just as unable to communicate her plight. As Ester is the intellectual fleeing from the physical side of life, Anna is fleeing from intelligence and consciousness into the void of sensuality. We see her going out into the street, picking up a young waiter, seducing him without joy, and we see slowly growing in her "the terror of drifting into the wash of incomprehensible sensuality."

Perhaps we are to see the two antagonistic sisters as the two elements in every woman: intelligence and consciousness rebelling against the physical limitations imposed by the woman's sexual role, and the enjoyment of the physical elements in life always obscured and limited by reflection or analysis of it. What is appropriate when joined—sensuality and consciousness—becomes destructive when separated. Jack Richardson has tried to interpret *The Silence* along these lines and has thus related Bergman to one of the basic themes of modern European art, "that the Spirit, the mind, and all they aspired to by way of order and peace, have been irreparably crippled by the knowledge that there is in life no principle but an unyielding sightless rhythm of sensuality."

Seeing Anna and Ester as one woman in two parts means that one can take the chief theme of the film as the nature of woman, and thus closer to *Wild Strawberries* and *The Virgin Spring* than to the first two parts of this trilogy, which are not really about woman at all. But to focus too exclusively on this theme, more subtle and more interesting as it may be, is to forget the strong emphasis on that old friend of Bergman, the problem of communication, carried in this film by the discussion of language and words.

The character of Anna's son brings us back to the theme of communication and words. He dallies briefly with some sort of sexual perversion (perhaps transvestism, as in the scene with the dwarfs), which is meant to parallel Anna's seduction of the waiter and Ester's self-abuse. And at the end he goes away with his mother, presumably leaving Ester alone to die. Ester leaves her nephew a list of the foreign words she has compiled. He has seen too much ever to be innocent again, and his legacy is a list of words he cannot understand. But the end, as in the two earlier films, is not without hope. Just as father and son briefly spoke together at the end of *Through a Glass Darkly,* just as the pastor continued to use the ancient religious words to a congregation composed wholly of the mistress whose love he had crushingly rejected, so there is not only the dying woman left alone, the broken child and sensuous mother falling into the abyss, there is the love of that mother for her child, the fruit of her body, part of the love she still has for her own body.

In these three films, Bergman is (like most of the death of God theologians themselves) obsessed by the problem of God. The protagonists cannot get hold of God, so they destroy themselves in madness, despair over their inability to love, or move inexorably toward physical and spiritual death. In these films, there is neither laughter nor delight, and thus the whole richness of life without God is not faced. But Bergman knows here that there are angels (as Polanski knows that there are devils) and that when you meet an angel the thing to do is to wrestle with it, even though you know you never can claim a decisive victory.

Recently, Bergman gave an interview in which he confessed that the making of these haunted films had brought him peace. The films do not portray that peace, but it is hard not to trust Bergman's confession. God has brought men peace, and so has the death of God.

When the presence of religion in my life faded away entirely, life at the same time became enormously easier to live.

Have you by chance read a marvelous essay by Sartre published in a rather stupid magazine, *Vogue,* I believe? In it he spoke of his blocks as an artist and as a writer. He suffered for a long time because what he was doing wasn't perfect. Then slowly, after thinking the whole thing carefully through, he realized that his insane anxiety about not creating worthwhile things was an atavism that stemmed from a religious notion, according to which there exists something that could be called the supreme good, or something created by man that would be perfect. When he discovered this atavism in himself, this survival of an idea giving credence to the existence of absolute, extreme perfection, when he brought this out into the light of day and was definitely rid of it, he immediately lost the blocks that were standing in the way of his creativity as an artist.

I had an experience that, oddly enough, was quite similar. When the religious superstructure that weighed heavily upon me crumbled and disappeared, the blocks that were standing in the way of my writing also vanished. I got rid of my inferiority complex as a writer. In particular, I got rid of the fear of not being modern, up-to-date. I did all this housecleaning when I made *The Communicants*. Since then, as far as what I've just been talking about is concerned, everything has been calm and right.

### Rosemary's Baby

The Legion of Decency gave *Rosemary's Baby* its lowest rating, but that was probably a severe theological error. Its condemnation was surely not theological, but either because of Mia Farrow's ritual nudity or because Pope Paul's visit to America was treated as a part of the New York entertainment scene, it offended the Legion of Decency. The theology of the film, in spite of the Marxism of Roman Polanski, is nearly orthodox: God is dead, and this is a horrible fact, and the demons will get you if you don't watch out. The nearest parallel in recent literature to the theology of this film is John Updike's *Couples* in which the author says all this hanky-panky is clearly inevitable since they're turning their backs on God.

This film is about the death of God, as the chief witch, Castavet, cries out in the final scene: "God is dead! God is dead and Satan lives! The year is One, the first year of our Lord! The year is One, God is done!" So part of the point of the film is to suggest the connection between the death of God and the emergence of the occult underground. Witchcraft, necromancy, astrology, the occult—all of these have indeed risen rapidly to the surface in the past several years. The astrology columns are no longer the refuge of the lonely, poor, and troubled. They are often the first part of the daily paper our college students turn to today.

But the central focus of the film is neither God nor witches but Jesus. Who shall our redeemer be in the time of the death of God? "Our hearts are our best prayer-rooms and the chaplains who can help us most are ourselves," Melville has written, but this is not the answer of Ira Levin's novel or Polanski's film.

The theme of the film is the new messiah, fathered by the devil (who may also be the pope) on Rosemary, the wife of a young actor. The young couple take a new apartment in New York City and fall in with some older and pleasant neighbors. As Rosemary's pregnancy goes along, and as the friends have set her up with their favorite obstetrician, it appears that the neighbors in fact head up a local coven of witches. Or do they? We are not quite sure at first, as Rosemary is not quite sure. But, with the help of a friend, Rosemary collects some volumes on witchcraft and discovers that her friend Castavet is in fact the son of a witch from Glasgow. And we nearly believe at the moment when Rosemary finally believes, in that extraordinary final scene, with (Rose) Mary and her infant in the cradle. The child is born and taken away from the mother. Rosemary stumbles into an adjoining apartment where the child rests in a black-draped bassinette and the visit of the wise men is being reenacted. Gathered around are visitors from many lands, bringing gifts—a nice touch, that.

Rosemary enters the nativity scene to claim her child and her own maternity. She is told that the paternity of the child is not as she imagines, and—like the first Mary—she rebels at the witch-angel's annunciation. In the final moment in the film she gently moves to the cradle, has a moment of horror as she looks at the infant's eyes, and then, at the end, gently smiles at the child which she accepts as her own. In Levin's novel, though not in the film, the assembled guests are shouting their ave marias, "Hail Rosemary." The implication of the final acceptance of the child is that this Mary, like the other one, will take her child and raise him well, only to lose him, as all mothers must, so he can set about his redemptive work. Castavet, at the end, in a striking

Magnificat, declares the new acceptable year of the new Lord, declaring that this child will rule the world and bring down the mighty from their seats.

This is a strange film and it gets much of its power from its ability to persuade us to believe something that really cannot be believed, that there really are nonmetaphorical witches. After all, if the gods are dead, then witches and devils are dead as well, and, like the gods, can come back into our language only as metaphors. But metaphors you only use; you do not believe them.

The other odd thing about *Rosemary's Baby* is that it is, for all of Polanski's Marxism, something of an anti-Marxist tract. The good life is still the civilized life of the city, apartment-hunting, shopping, trying to get ahead, and having babies. The alternative to this life is obedience to the new messiah.

But perhaps when the old gods die a new messiah is not really needed. There are not messiahs, new or old, in Bergman's trilogy, but we heard him confess that he came to a rest and a peace by becoming his own messiah. The old Jesus, demessianized, without his traditional letters of recommendation, may still serve. Along with this, or perhaps instead of this, Bergman's way to peace may be our own. "The Chaplains who can help us most are ourselves." Melville deserves to have the last word.

NOTES

1. Dwight MacDonald, in *Esquire* 58, no. 2 (August 1962), pp. 116-17.
2. Stanley Kauffmann, in *The New Republic* 148, no. 19 (May 11. 1963).

# 6

# Bergman's Vision of
# Good and Evil

Anthony Schillaci

In the film *Prison* (Fangelse, 1948) one of Ingmar Bergman's characters makes the statement, "If one can believe in God, there is no problem; if one cannot, there is no solution." Although some present these words as Bergman's philosophy of life, they hardly describe the condition of his characters, for it is their peculiar torment that they *do* believe in God and still have a problem. The problem which they share with their creator is the enigma of evil in the world. For these individuals, the single greatest challenge to belief in the existence of a good God is the presence of evil in the world he is said to have created. Almost the entire body of Ingmar Bergman's recent films has taken up the challenge of this problem.

*Evil Everywhere*

Critics are fond of citing Bergman's family background as the son of an Evangelical Lutheran pastor to explain his preoccupation with evil. Whether the inference is true or not, there is no doubting the emphasis on evil in the works of the leading Swedish director. Even his early films on romantic love and the problems of marriage show a singular fascination with evil, sometimes in human foibles, at other times with evil personified—the Devil. One of his rather sophisticated entertainments is entitled *The*

*Devil's Eye,* after the Swedish proverb, "A chaste woman is a sty in the Devil's eye." The earlier film, *Prison,* shows the Devil ruling the world which, unknown to us, is hell itself.

In a sense, however, these films are not typical of their period in the director's art. For the most part the films made up until 1956 explore in a comic vein the difficulties of married life and largely resolve themselves by affirming the necessity of compromise in marriage. Reconciliations of this sort appear in *Lesson in Love, Sawdust and Tinsel,* and *Smiles of a Summer Night.* It is only with the appearance of *The Seventh Seal,* an apocalyptic work that won Bergman international recognition, that the director takes up the problems of good and evil, and he does so in the context of man's relations with God.

Ingmar Bergman's statement, "To me, religious problems are continuously alive," is well known to his critics and followers. The intimate relation between his art and the religious milieu, moreover, can be deduced from another remark of his: "Art lost its creative drive the moment it was separated from worship." This is obviously Bergman the dramatist speaking. And yet, although he has not embarked upon a contemporary restoration of the medieval mystery and morality plays, Bergman does come closer than almost any other film artist to creating similar plays for modern man. If we examine briefly *The Seventh Seal, The Virgin Spring, Through a Glass Darkly, Winter Light,* and *The Silence,* we can examine the form that this ancient genre has taken in the hands of an artist tormented by his unique and fascinating vision of good and evil.

Merely to list these five films is to reveal the range and complexity of the director's talents. They range from the medieval allegories of *The Seventh Seal* and *The Virgin Spring* to the bleak realism of *Winter Light* and *Through a Glass Darkly.* Through each, Bergman conducts his search for a solution to the mystery of iniquity, ending with the extreme abstraction of *The Silence.* Even more startling than the brilliance and variety of the director's forms is their seeming morbidity: a chess game with Death in time of plague in *The Seventh Seal;* a rape-murder and brutal vengeance in *The Virgin Spring*; and a trilogy that deals in incest and lesbianism, disbelief and autoeroticism, suicide, adultery, and perversion. We should be careful, however, of charging Bergman with a sick view of the world, lest he reply in the words of the Painter in *The Seventh Seal* who, when criticized for choosing so grisly a subject as the dance of Death, says the following:

JONS: Why do you paint such nonsense?
PAINTER: I thought it would serve to remind people they must die.
JONS: Well, it's not going to make them feel any happier.
PAINTER: Why should one always make people happy? It might not be a bad idea to scare them a little once in a while.
JONS: If you do scare them . . .
PAINTER: They'll think.

Bergman's films may constitute a crazy dance of death for modern man, but it is not without meaning. The director is not morbid, but simply wishes to make us think. Instead of comforting the afflicted he wishes to afflict the comfortable. The means he chooses is to give us his own reflections on the presence of evil in the world, his own vision of good and evil, which he incarnates in the visual medium of the cinema.

## Good with Evil

How can we characterize this vision of Sweden's leading film genius? We can say, first off, that in Bergman's view evil is not the sole reality. Whatever the charges of morbid preoccupation, evil never appears unrelieved but is always mixed with the good, as the cockle with the wheat in the Gospel story.

To list the content of evil in the films we are about to examine is to caricature them, as if we were to describe the content of Shakespeare's plays as greed, ambition, imprudence, and jealousy. Bergman's films present the world as it really is, beset by many serious evils and failings. To present a world other than this one—the never-never land of Hollywood's clever, affluent people living in untroubled euphoria—would be to distort reality. Bergman chooses instead to make us see reality as it is.

In *The Seventh Seal* the Knight plays chess with Death for the highest stakes, his life. Around him, heavy and pervasive as the disillusionment of the Crusades, there lies the plague, religious hysteria, death of every kind. But none of this miasma of evil is so telling as the Knight's own personal evil, the religious doubts that make it impossible for him either to live with God, as the players Jof and Mia, or without him, as his squire, Jons. The film tells its story in light and shadow, presenting them as symbolically inseparable. Clad in black, Death appears in the gray dawn of the seashore and speaks to the Knight only in shadow. Jof and Mia, on the other hand, are bathed in light, both when they first appear and at the end of the film, when the silhouettes of the doomed dance off, holding hands with Death. Always what is most important is not the contrast of good and bad characters but the light and darkness in each warring for domination. The Knight, in spite of the stench of the plague and the bitter memory of the Crusades, is modern man crying out in the false confessional.

Why can't I kill God within me? Why does He live on in this painful and humiliating way even though I curse Him and want to tear Him out of my heart? . . . I want knowledge, not faith, not suppositions, but knowledge.

Afflicted as he is by doubt, there is more to the Knight's character than the wound of God's silent presence. He resolves to use his reprieve from Death for one meaningful deed, and the rescue of Jof and Mia from the plague is the fruit of his resolution. Even his cynical squire, Jons, a born skeptic, acts to rescue the girl and Jof from their tormentors. No one, it appears, is beyond redemption.

Nowhere does the baffling mixture of good and evil in men appear more dramatically than in *The Virgin Spring*. A young girl on her way to Mass is raped and killed by three thieving goatherds in the woods. When fate places them in his hands, the father takes ruthless vengeance on the murderers in one of the most horrifying scenes in contemporary cinema. Here is evil enough, with a wily serving-wench (carrying an illegitimate child) placing a curse on the maiden as she leaves for Mass. And yet, the simplicity of the medieval tale of innocence destroyed is misleading, particularly if we note the development of the characters. The victim, spoiled by her parents and vain over her blonde beauty, is not so innocent, and she plays the coquette with disastrous effects. On the other hand, the younger brother of the goatherds, though innocent of their crime, falls at the hands of the avenging father. Even the mother, for all her piety, is not without fault, for she is guilty of denying life, refusing love to her spouse. But the most shocking mixture of all is that of the girl's father who, in spite of a nominal Christianity, acts out a ritual of pagan vengeance and proves himself worse than the lecherous murderers of his child.

The pattern of intermingled good and evil that emerges from these somber visual dramas develops as it repeats itself in the famous trilogy. *Through a Glass Darkly* presents a popular novelist who has systematically rejected his children out of a callous preoccupation with himself. So cold is he that he can watch with professional fascination, and record in his diary, the progress of his daughter's hopeless schizophrenia. In fact, it is the accidental reading of this entry that drives Karin so far into insanity that she seduces her brother in a striking scene that takes place in the shattered hull of a wrecked ship, the symbol of the ravaged family. And the one responsible for so much evil, the hollow novelist, finds that he is able to turn from its horror and make an overture to his son.

Similar in structure, *Winter Light* presents a village pastor who has lost his faith and assuaged his emptiness by entering a loveless affair with the plain schoolteacher who is so far beneath him. He reaches bottom, when, unable to console a depressed parishioner, he learns that the man has committed suicide. It takes a venal and ignorant sexton to remind the pastor of Christ's despair on the cross, so that he can summon up the courage to intone the first psalm of Evensong. As in the case of the novelist, death has not completed his work in this man so long as he is willing to make a new beginning.

*The Silence,* a film far more complex, brilliant, and well conceived than its companions in the trilogy, paints the light and shadow within man in more cinematic terms than the others. A special developing process gives the film's deep-focus, black and white photography an almost tactile quality. Here are close-ups in which the chiaroscuro of the human face speaks of the forces working within the soul. The heavy, almost overpowering silence of the film provides a vacuumlike setting for a multiplicity of evils: a country at war, with communications destroyed and violence in the streets; the aunt, Ester, dying of a revolting consumptive disease; the sensual sister, Anna, coupling animalistically with the silent waiter.

What makes the film an advance in Bergman's conception of the problem at hand is the symbolic signification of the sisters and their relationships. It seems evident that these are not individual persons but fragments of one human nature. The very distortions and exaggerated actions highlight the evil of a false dichotomy between the analytical-intellectual side of human nature, and its sensual-intuitive function. The lesbian relationship then becomes meaningful as a desire for wholeness, now made horrible by the excesses resulting from their alienation: Ester's autoeroticism and drunkenness; Anna's wanton promiscuity and narcissistic sensuality. Whereas the film director had been content in other films to show the mixture of good and evil in each human, here he boldly splits humanity open, shattering its unity with the malady of the age, the separation and isolation of sense and sensibility, intellect and emotionality, objectivity and subjectivity. Separated and only half-human, the sisters both turn to a sterile caricature of love which is fruitless, bearing neither offspring nor personal fulfillment.

These are the images and actions which blend and separate evil and good within man in Bergman's films. It is almost impossible by description to capture the visual power with which this view is conveyed in the remarkable films of the director. In their totality, they resolve the dilemma of the central character in *Joan of the Angels*, Father Joseph, who fails to see that an honest view of the evil within us would eliminate the cowardly need to personify evil in the form of a "diabolical" possession. Unlike Bunuel, Bergman refuses to view reality with evil as the uncontested ruler of human destiny. While he is, at times, ruthless in his portrayal of their inauthenticity, he never makes excuses for the characters and he never denies their humanity. In fact, Bergman affirms the admixture of good and evil as part of that human condition of which he is so acute an observer. There is no simple dismissal of either element in reality, for maturity consists in realizing that we must expect to find the two mingled: light and dark, authentic and inauthentic, creative and destructive, good and evil. The symbol which best embodies this first insight into the problem of evil is the moving one from *The Virgin Spring*. The envious serving girl, Ingeri, reluctantly preparing the lunch for Karin's journey to Mass, hollows out a loaf of bread, greedily wolfing down its contents, and places in it an ugly toad. Later, it is at the precise moment that Karin offers this loaf to the lecherous goatherds that mischief is unleashed and the rape-murder committed. The loaf falls apart and there the toad sits obscenely in the center of the white bread. Like it or no, this is the world as it really is—a good marred by the mystery of evil.

## God's Silence

Where is God in this world groaning under the incubus of evil? We have already noted the statement from Bergman's 1948 film, *Prison*: "If one can believe in God, there is no problem." The director creates characters who for the most part either do believe or at least wish to believe as the Knight in *The Seventh Seal* complains, "What is going to happen to those of us who want to believe but are not able to? And what is to become of those who neither want to nor are capable of believing?" The problem is this: Although men desire to believe, the pervasive presence of evil in the world, like an obscene smog hanging over mankind, prevents men from seeing the clear sky and the heavenly bodies. When he is overwhelmed by the evil within, man in Bergman's universe looks to God and challenges him almost as Job arguing with his Creator. The father in *The Virgin Spring* articulates the anguish of man over God's silence in the presence of evil. After coming upon his daughter's body he flails about in blind fury, then stops and raises his fists to heaven: "You saw it, God. You saw it! The death of an innocent child, and my vengeance. You permitted it, and I don't understand you."

The cry is a familiar one. We have already recalled the Knight's anguish that he can't kill God within him, and so he must live, somehow, with the silence of God. The schizoid daughter in *Through a Glass Darkly* summons up a horrifying image of God as a spider who tries to attack her sexually. It is difficult to tell, in her illness, whether this view of God stems from her rejection by her father, who is unable to love, or whether it constitutes a personal rejection of love signified by the perverse substitution of incest. In either case, the evil overwhelms man, and God remains silent. He is like her husband whom she tells, "You always do the right thing, and it is never any good."

In *Winter Light* the image changes from the isolated island on which the family summer home is located (accessible only by boat or the ambiguous helicopter) to a visual reduction of all life to the gray tones of a winter day. The light is gone because Faith has died, and so God is no longer present within. The pastor, crushed by his inability to help his pitiful flock, unable even to feel grief over the suicide of the fisherman, takes cold comfort from his sexton's remark that even Christ was misunderstood by his friends. There is a significant development here in the silence of God when even his intimates are unable to understand his communications. The film's ending may indicate, as Stanley Kauffmann has suggested, that Bergman and his characters are now concerned not so much with finding God as with finding a way to live with his memory. This theme of memory, placing God in the past like a vague nostalgia or a sweet souvenir, recurs in *The Silence,* the last film to develop the seeming indifference of God to evil.

The Swedish version of the script for *The Silence* is explicit in its reference to "the silence of God." We learn early in the film, for example, that the father of the two sisters, a dominant figure, has died. Not only is God dead, then, but the film finds no substitute for him, being almost devoid of a fully developed man in its ambience. There is only the child, observing endlessly and inscrutably, and the sensuous waiter, who only knows how to satisfy his considerable appetite. Perhaps the most direct comment on God in this film appears in the person of the manservant, a kind of butler who ministers to Ester in her illness. Kindly, solicitous, efficient in his services, but unable to communicate, he is the epitome of irrelevance and ineffectuality. He represents organized religion, reduced to a pious institution of social services associated with the ornate hotel, a symbol of the empty past and the *Weltbild* of its deformed inhabitants. The butler shows pictures of a loved one who has died (Christ, God) to the boy, but the child rejects and hides them under the hotel corridor carpeting. Anna and Ester are left to loneliness and death, with nothing more than the distant tolling of a church bell or the menacing roar of the prowling tank to break the godless silence.

In one way or another, then, each of the films shows men suffering the evils of their condition with the burden of God's silence hanging over their lives. Unable to answer the problem of evil, they are destroyed or mutilated by it themselves: the dance of Death in *The Seventh Seal*; the brutal vengeance of the father in *The Virgin Spring*; Anna's madness in *Through a Glass Darkly*; the quiet despair of the pastor in *Winter Light*; and finally Ester's inevitable, lonely death in Timokas, the mysterious land whose name is etymologically related to the word "executioner" in Estonian. This is the somber picture presented by Bergman, a canvas not unlike those of Hieronymous Bosch. Is this the full extent of the director's conception of good and evil or can we read the data of his film tragedies further than we have already done?

## Accepting Evil

It is not at all clear that Bergman has proffered an answer to the reason for evil in the world. This is obviously the case if by "answer" we mean a solution to the problem of evil and therefore of God's existence. Is there perhaps an answer in the larger sense, more acceptable to our generation, of finding some means of

continuing to live amidst evil? Bergman himself has commented
upon his trilogy, suggesting that today it is not God, but the sim-
pler issue of choosing between suicide and acceptance of life
which preoccupies him. It is acceptance that he claims to have
affirmed in his films.

Although we need not agree with the director's estimate of his
art, we can verify his statement as far as it does explain his works.
In *The Virgin Spring,* the father does receive an answer to his
questioning challenge of God. It is an answer echoed in the other
films that deal with the theme of good and evil and with God's
existence. After his agonizing confession of ignorance of God, the
father nevertheless bends his knees and, with an effort as great
as that expended in uprooting the birch sapling, he says, "Yet I
now ask you for forgiveness—I do not know of any other way to
reconcile myself with my own hands. I don't know of any other
way to live." Man must continue to exist, to accept life with its
evils and live. This message of hope in a minor key provides a
resolution for so many Bergman films that we have come to recognize it as his signature, like Fellini's bleak dawns and Antonioni's
lonely landscapes. A critic has asked wryly, "If this trilogy is
Bergman's idea of accepting life, one wonders what he would give
us if he rejected it." [1] But MacDonald seems to have gone very
little beyond the surface meaning of Bergman's solution of acceptance. What makes the resolution of the films we have analyzed
more satisfying than a nonrejection of life is their precious spark
of genuine hope. The characters are compelled by their suffering
to assert their humanity, to accept and love it, and in this they
(and we) become a little more human. If there is a good that
comes out of the evil it is this acceptance which completes Bergman's vision of the mystery of iniquity.

In almost every instance there is a good which mysteriously
emerges from the chaos of disorder. The Knight in *The Seventh
Seal* uses his reprieve from death "for one meaningful deed," the
saving of Jof, Mia, and the child from the plague. But he signifi-
cantly does more than this. He lessens the suffering of the witch
condemned to burn, and leads, as well, the wretched band follow-

ing him to the castle, where they can recognize Death as the envoy of God. The immense power of that scene, the darkest in the film and yet radiant with light, is unforgettable. Each in his turn, Plog the smith, Jons the squire, the girl, the Knight and his wife, courteously and calmly greet Death, whom we do not see except in their acceptance of him. Gone is the violent fear of the flagellants and the hysterical gaiety of the revelers. Peaceful acceptance is the gesture, as in the background Antonius Block, the knight-crusader, prays, "Have mercy on us because we are small and frightened and ignorant." Even the squire, "under protest," as he says, kneels. In the very last scene, in the shelter of a great tree which looks down on the shining sea, brilliant in the sunlight, Jof and Mia with the child watch the dance of Death. As Jof identifies the figures silhouetted against the sky he says, "And Death, the severe master, invites them to dance . . . a solemn dance toward the dark lands, while the rain washes their faces and cleans the salt of their tears from their cheeks." The reference to the Apocalypse is significant, for it was from this book that the wife was reading when Death made his call. The contemporary revelation, however, made in purely visual terms of great beauty, is Bergman's.

It is a salvific rain, similar to that described by Jof, which breaks the silence that engulfed the sisters, Ester and Anna, in the last film of the trilogy. After the final clash between them, the onanism and lust ending in Ester's inevitable death, hope is found in the fact that the journey to their father's house continues. As they travel, Anna lowers the train window to bathe her face and breast in a purifying rain. The child is the most cogent argument of hope. He no longer has to choose between the fragments of humanity: between sterile, diseased intellectuality and narcissistic sensuality. For once indifferent to his mother's sensual presence, he studies the first words of the mysterious language spoken in Timoka: "heart" and "hand." His large eyes no longer reflect innocence, for he has seen too much, but they manifest something of more value—understanding.

The note of hope in the first two films of the trilogy is muffled, but it is there. The first, true to its title, presents Bergman's view of good and evil "through a glass, darkly." The reference to St. Paul's ode to Charity from Corinthians is intentional. Although the film suffers from a confusion of emphasis on the schizophrenic daughter, it ends by resolving the condition of the novelist father. For the first time he reaches out and communicates with the son, who is shattered by his monstrous experience and his sister's final madness. He tells the boy that there is a basis for reality. It *is* the giving and receiving of love. Out of the evil union and frightening vision of the "spider god" comes redemption in the form of a renewed ability to communicate in love. *Winter Light* is darker, if anything, than its predecessor. Nevertheless, out of the sordid, loveless affair with the teacher, and the suicide of the fisherman, comes the ability to identify with Christ on the cross and therefore somehow to carry on in the dark night of unbelief. The courage required to face an empty church and begin Evensong with the psalm, "The earth is full of the glory of God," is no small grace and the pastor receives it with the full dignity of his suffering. Like the novelist, he has accepted his humanity and may eventually come to live with it.

We have reserved until last *The Virgin Spring* and its own unique reflection of Bergman's vision of good emerging from evil in human life. The reason is that this film seems the most complete statement on the problem available to us in Bergman's works. Fully conceived in visual terms, *The Virgin Spring* reinforces with strong images the simple poetry of its narrative. The father of the murdered girl, after accusing God of looking down in indifference upon the rape-killing and his own vengeance, asks forgiveness. His answer comes in the sudden appearance of a spring which gushes forth when he and Mareta lift Karin's body from the ground. Water once more signifies redemption, as it did in the healing rain of *The Seventh Seal* and *The Silence,* and in the brilliant image of Jof and Mia by the sea after Death has passed. The healing that comes in *The Virgin Spring* takes place in those who survive the young girl. Ingeri, the pagan servant who placed Odin's curse on the maiden, now bends and bathes, then drinks from the virgin spring, all the concentrated malice draining from her face. Mareta, the girl's mother, confesses to her husband, as they race toward the scene of the slaying, "I love her too much, Tore, more than God himself. And when I saw that she turned more to you than to me, I began to hate you. It is I who am punished with this, Tore. It is I who am guilty. . . ."

But it is Tore himself, the strong father who radiated the dignity of a god, who changes most in his realization that his crime of vengeance is worse than anything worked by the destructive passion of the ignorant goatherds. Impressive as he was with his head bowed in grace over the meal, in the anguish of his loss he reverted to the pre-Christian code of revenge. There are few sequences in contemporary cinema to equal the ritual purification of Tore for his pagan deed as he bathes, dresses himself in finery, and takes the slaughtering knife (the sword is for equals) to kill with cold, dispassionate malice the sleeping goatherds. This deed, more than the innocent maiden's death, shows the admixture of good and evil in the human soul. As soon as Tore realizes this, he shakes his head in wonder at God's permission of his crime, then repents and promises to build a church, a new affirmation of the Christian faith, as his penance. It is not the church, but the new wholeness which he finds with Mareta that verifies the good outcome symbolized in the virgin spring.

### Bergman's Compelling Call

This, then, is Bergman's vision of good and evil, his own private heaven and hell. It is told with an imagery and visual poetry which constitute a major contribution to the art of the cinema. One mark of the authenticity of the vision is its refusal to present a facile solution to the problem of evil. Basically, Bergman is saying that coexistence of good and evil is the best we can hope for from our fragmented humanity. Raising the question as he does, in the context of a challenge to God's existence, the Swedish director's films speak very much with the accents of contemporary man. If these films did nothing more than help man to express his agonized longing for wholeness, they would justify themselves.

But more than this, they articulate his spiritual striving at the same time that they encourage him to accept his fallen humanity. This contribution makes of Bergman's films true art, and the most complete reincarnation of the medieval morality play available to us. Although they do not teach "moral" solutions, their beautiful truth nevertheless gives the viewer a compelling call to become more fully human and therefore more fully and wholly a person. More and more, by directors such as Ingmar Bergman, we are invited to look for our image in the cinema, to seek our identity in this mirror of reality, and to refresh ourselves in the shimmering reflections of the art that writes with light.

## NOTES

1. Dwight MacDonald, *On Movies* (Englewood Cliffs, N.J.: Prentice-Hall, 1969), p. 418.

# 7

# The Purpose of the
# Grotesque in Fellini's Films

Harvey G. Cox, Jr.

On the way out to see Fellini I found myself secretly hoping we might have a flat tire or run out of gas. Ostensibly I was in Rome at an international conference on "The Culture of Unbelief" sponsored jointly (would you believe?) by the Vatican and the University of California at Berkeley. Before I left Harvard for the trip I had been asked by an American friend in Rome what I'd like to do there. I answered (only 50 percent facetiously) by saying, "I'd like to meet Fellini." Now we were on the way out to Cinecitta where Fellini was filming *Satyricon.* And I was getting cold feet. Why?

I don't like my idols to have feet of clay. More precisely, if they do have clay feet I'd rather not know it. And my attitude toward Fellini came pretty close to idolatry. We theologians claim that idolatry is the projection of one's own fantasies, weaknesses, hopes, and fears, real or imagined, on someone or something larger and more powerful. The Hebrew prophets denounced idolatry because it is really a form of self-worship. Maybe so. But I am a little more tolerant of idols than most people are—just as long as you *know* they're idols and when you fall down and worship them you know it is all part sham. Please, Federico, may your feet be flesh.

As we careened through the April streets of Rome, with Eileen Hughes at the wheel (a *Time-Life* writer and a Rome resident now writing a book on Fellini), another ironic tableau briefly titillated my mind. In one of Fellini's earliest films, *The White Sheik* (1952), an ingenuous young couple come to Rome. He is lit up by the expectation of using his Roman relatives' contacts to get in to see the Pope. She, however, wants to meet "The White Sheik," hero of her favorite photo-comic strip. Instant cut: Me in Rome, now, but with *both* those hopes, and it looked as though I might cop a daily double. I was there at the Vatican's expense, via a generous grant from the Agnelli Foundation (the Fiat loot), but if it had really come down to a choice between meeting *il poeta* or *il pape,* Fellini or Montini, the infallible Head of the True Church or the Biggest Liar in Rome (as the Pope and Fellini respectively describe themselves), I secretly know what my choice would have been: When it comes to *vita,* I prefer *La Dolce* to *Humana.*

We had two close calls and did run out of gas and had to change cars, but we finally made it to Cinecitta where Fellini was filming Trimalchio's feast for his new movie version of Petronius's *Satyricon.* As we climbed out of our Fiat, the omnipresent symbol of the largesse of my host, the set was being prepared for the afternoon shooting. Gleaming sides of beef and mutton hung from the walls of a movie-set Roman kitchen of DeMille proportions. A cageful of snarling dogs slobbered at the teams of panicky technicians, indolent extras, and curious visitors with which Fellini loves to surround himself when he is shooting. The great man himself had not yet arrived, so Eileen and I chatted with assorted cameramen, script girls, and hangers-on. To my discomfort, Eileen invariably told everyone we met that I was in Rome as a guest of the Vatican. Knowing something about Rome's traditional and virulent (and perfectly justifiable) anticlericalism, I always inwardly shuddered at this kind of introduction. I thought it would guarantee a fishy stare or a cold shoulder. It didn't. Part of the reason was that the Italian papers had been playing up the conference I was attending. It was somewhat epochal since it had brought together, under papal sponsorship, atheists (including some communists), Christians, and scholars of religion from various backgrounds. The tabloids had especially featured some remarks I had dropped at the opening session which were interpreted as being very critical of the church. For a couple of days I had found myself, like Marcello in *La Dolce Vita,* set upon by the *paparazzi* and the unbelievably ingenious Roman press corps. I was a kind of mini-celebrity, at least for forty-eight hours, and enjoyed every minute of it.

Also, the Italians I met, and this includes Fellini, are *not,* to put it mildly, indifferent to religion. Some of them, especially the most strident atheists, seem almost obsessed with it. Fellini's pictures include an enormous range of religious themes and personages, from the swindlers dressed like priests in *Il Bidone* and the processions in *La Strada* and *Cabiria,* to the dangling statue of Christ that opens *La Dolce Vita.* Italy is a country where Catholicism resides not in the head but in the entrails. Everybody has not just a strong opinion about Christianity but fevered feelings as well.

The set for *Satyricon* looked like a combined psychiatric ward and freaks' convention. Fellini has always had a fascination with grotesque-looking people. In *Satyricon* his thing about monstrosities has exceeded all bounds. The area was seething with midgets, gigantic black-as-coal extras decked out as Nubian slaves, acrobats, dwarfs, cretinous-looking recruits from the Roman stockyards whom Fellini had picked up because he thought they looked like real ancient Romans, a seven-foot giant, and an assortment of the fattest ladies I have seen since I visited the circus sideshow as a kid. Fellini simply cannot resist eye-grabbing people and has been known to sidle up to really odd-looking types on the streets and offer them jobs in his movies. Some of his associates thought he pushed it too far when he arrived at the *Satyricon* set a few weeks before, bringing with him an armless and legless man he affectionately referred to as "the torso." But Fellini does not use grotesques in his films just for shock or sensation. He is really very fond of them, and they sense it in him. They do not work for

Fellini just for money; they seem to realize instinctively that they mean something special to him and that through them he is saying something to his audiences. But what?

Some critics think Fellini's use of the grotesque grows out of his interest in character versus plot. The French film critic Gilvert Salachas, for example, says that by creating characters who exaggerate certain tendencies Fellini is actually entering a judgment against them, though never a very severe one, a kind of *ad absurdum* argument that Fellini enjoys but never brings to completion because he has too much sympathy for screwballs and is notoriously indulgent toward charlatans. That might be so, but it hardly explains Fellini's obvious proclivity for bizarre-*looking* people. My own conviction is that *il poeta* populates his sets with monstrosities and galoots partly just because they are just *visually* interesting. He revels in them for the same reason he likes curvaceous women with ample backsides (like Sandra Milo and Anita Ekberg), splendid silk costumes, festive orgies, parades and scenes with sharply contrasting shapes and colors. Fellini thinks with his eyes, which is one reason he is so great.

But he also likes bizarre-looking people in his movies for a more subtle reason. In a recent essay a theological colleague of mine discussed Flannery O'Connor's short stories as an attempt to use the grotesque in order to recover our lost sense of the mysterious, the transcendent, and the holy. I think the same impulse is at work in Fellini. But such a brash remark, exuding as it does the *odium theologicum*, deserves a couple lines of defense.

Here goes: It is my conviction that conventional religion has declined in Western society *not* because of the advance of science, the spread of education, or any of the reasons normally advanced for secularization. It has declined mainly because the tight, bureaucratic instrumental model of society on which we have been fed since the industrial revolution renders us incapable of experiencing those nonrational dimensions of existence on which religion is based. The absurd, the inspiring, the uncanny, the awesome, the terrifying, the ecstatic—none of these fit well in a production-

and-efficiency-oriented society. Although the blame for this is usually hung on something called "puritanism" or "the Protestant ethic," I think that analysis is too superficial. We are now learning that the building of an industrial society can be blessed by any number of ideologies, sacred and secular.

The fact is that Christianity, especially in its Protestant form, was conned into providing the spiritual cement and stick-and-carrot values for Western industrialization. Willingly conned perhaps, but conned nevertheless. As Fellini knows so well, and shows time after time in his films, the con man and the victim are really coconspirators. "Economic development," whatever that really is, and not Christianity, is the real religion of the Western world today. Our sacred grail is the growth of the GNP. Instead of dispatching Scripture-spouting missionaries to benighted lands, we now send them "developers" quoting chapter and verse from Rostow's *Stages of Economic Growth.* Christianity is not alone in having been taken in, used (and to some extent paid off) by the Moloch of production and efficiency. In other places on the globe communism, nationalism, and other ideologies have entered into the same plot.

The consequence of all this, as we begin to recognize the incalculable psychic damage industrial society inflicts on us as the price for its affluence, is that people all over the world are turning, sometimes a little desperately, to the overlooked corners of the culture, the nooks and crevices that were never completely absorbed into the Big Machine. Hence our fascination with the junk and rejects of the industrial process, and with the slippery stuff that never found a place in it, like astrology, madness, drugs, non-Western religions, mysticism. Even the current preoccupation with sex and violence can to some extent be understood on this basis. Both blood and sperm are explosive, irregular, feeling-pitched, messy, and irrationally fascinating. Neither can be safely stored in the smoothly humming memory bank of an IBM 270, to be printed out only when needed in the program. None of these forces are *containable* in the conventional, socially imposed receptacles our society builds into us to order and rationalize our experience. To use a theological term, they *transcend* conventional experience.

They can be manipulated, too, and that is very scary. We see every day the way industrial society uses not only religion but also sex and violence to undergird its own values and objectives. We are not only told to go to church so our minds will be calmed and our spirits rejuvenated (for better production on Monday), we are sold Hondas and Tareytons with boobs and asses, and violence has become a fast-moving commodity on which Those In Control are desperately trying to retain their near monopoly. Even astrology, alas, is not beyond bribing. Last week the papers reported that while he was in the British Intelligence Service during World War II, Ian Fleming paid the two horoscope advisers of Rudolf Hess to get him to fly to England and win the war. He flew to England but was put in jail. *Sic transit gloria stellae.*

Fellini digs grotesque people because he sees, much more vividly than the rest of us do, that our gleaming-geared industrial culture, for all its spectacular accomplishments, is also sick (fallen? damned?). He savors any sign of a reality that won't be contained in it. Sexy women distract us from our work; fat ladies don't fit in costumes; dwarfs and giants defy the standard sizes of beds and doorways; armless people embarrass us when it comes to offering them a cigarette. Fellini peppers his films with people like this because they are signs of Something Else (he never allows himself to say quite what)—a Something that just won't be packaged by the Container Corporation of America.

Fellini may never have read either Nietzsche or Buber. It doesn't really matter. His vision of the grotesque does make a contribution to a continuing battle they represent. Do we become human by an infinite escalation of the Self, or by an encounter with something terrifyingly and awesomely Other? *Ubermensch* or *I and Thou*? Buber opted for the latter and so does Fellini. Not only that: for Fellini (if I grok him aright), when we really allow ourselves to grapple with that awful Other, it turns out not to be demonic but, yes, gracious. Who will save us if we slip so completely into the slick, media-created soft life that we can no longer hear the voice of the sensuous angel calling to us playfully from across the rivulet?

Back to Cinecitta. Fellini appeared. I smiled casually and tried to look calm. (Later that week I was to see *why*, psychologically, Catholics kiss the pope's ring. It is *something* to *do* in the difficult moment.)

Fellini was Fellini. He wore a black, light-wool sweater and slacks. Around his neck hung a small scene-framer. He seemed calmly undisturbed by the hectic preparations still churning on around him. Eileen of course introduced me as "an American theologian, from Harvard, here at the Vatican conference" and so forth. Fellini shook my hand, shot me a glance that combined an instant sizing-up and a not-too-manufactured amiability, diluted with caution. Eileen went on with the introduction in her superb Italian. One out of every three words I could understand, and when she came to the part that revealed I was a *Protestant* theologian, Fellini suddenly looked interested. *Vive la grotesque!*

To an Italian, a Protestant theologian must be a little like a Tibetan endocrinologist or a Portuguese vegetarian. No, not quite. A lot of Italians, especially Romans, think of themselves as very religious, even maybe very Christian, but very, very anticlerical. For eons Romans have carried on an incestuous love-hate duel with *il pape* and with Catholicism in general. Fellini is no exception. Maybe, in a theologian who was, however, not a Catholic, there might be something of that fat lady whose bosom exceeds the largest bra size or the midget whose arms are too short to work on the assembly line. For Italians, to sum it up briefly, a Protestant theologian is a *really* marginal figure, with all the exotic charisma that entails.

Maybe Fellini didn't think that all at once, maybe not at all. But he did relax perceptibly, had one of his devotees pour us both a brandy, and started to tell me about his affection for the Milan Jesuits—who had supported *La Dolce Vita* after a Vatican organ had condemned it—and his contempt for Montini (now Paul VI, then Bishop of Milan) for suppressing those same Jesuits. I

remembered that Jesuit journal's review and was a little surprised
that Fellini had liked it. I remember thinking then that the breth-
ren had gone a little off the deep end to praise *La Dolce Vita* as a
highly moral and religious film, a film in fact even somewhat
puritanical in its depiction of Marcello's fleshy stumbling slide
into hades. My own view was that Fellini was a little more tolerant
of the flesh than they thought and that in the end, though we
might have wanted Marcello to pull himself together, we could
really understand why he didn't. As Salachas says of the way
Fellini treats his characters' weaknesses, "He always pleads exten-
uating circumstances."

Fellini was now going at great length in Italian. Eileen was
translating nobly and, at the same time, trying to get down this
anecdote in her brimming notebook of Felliniana. Later she
admitted to me what I suspected then—she often brings people
she thinks may interest Fellini to the set, because they spark him
to recall incidents she's never heard him relate before.

Of course she also thrives on meeting such people, and they
enjoy the whole scenario too, so everybody gets his kicks from
the arrangement. Of course, later on Eileen will have to cope with
the known fact that Fellini, the biggest liar in Rome (a tough
league to compete in), is fully capable of inventing whole incidents from his past and recounting them with the verisimilitude
of a painstaking biographer. For years, for example, he has been
telling people that during World War II he toured Italy with a
troupe of second-rate actors under the direction of Aldo Fabrizi,
and that his fascination with traveling performers dates in part
from that time. Fabrizi smilingly denies that any such tour ever
occurred. Once Fellini promised to hold a press conference and
clear the matter up, but he never did.

Fellini loves fantasy. Like the Italian pedestrian who would
rather make up elaborate, hand-waving answers when you ask
him for directions, rather than admit he doesn't know the address
you're looking for, Fellini hates to disappoint anyone who believes
he's lived a colorful, varied, and romantic life. In one of his
accounts of the tour with Fabrizi he even has five of the lady

players falling in love with him and thus causing enormous friction in the company. Fellini's notorious story about his running away to the circus as a lad may not be true either, at least outside Federico's head. But who cares? The important thing is that out of his undeniable fascination with tightrope walkers, hypnotists, fortune-tellers, traveling musicians, and the rest Fellini has conjured a world beyond realism and neorealism. It is a world that reminds us that what we often so baldly call "reality" may be a shoddy surrogate for the real thing.

I listened to Fellini's story about Montini, shaking my head and clucking sympathetically at the appropriate places. Still, I knew we were fencing and somehow I wanted to talk. I was apprehensive about asking Fellini a theological question. His films have been so overanalyzed by theologians that I am sure, like Bergman, he takes delight in tossing in a symbol here and there to throw the theological bloodhounds off the track while he slyly sloshes through streams and swamps where no symbol analyzer can follow. I also remembered the American chick in *8½* who bugs Guido, the director, with a question about whether the film he is making deals with "the Catholic conscience." So I tried something else.

"My question is really not very theological," I said, "but maybe it is." Fellini waited. "The angel in *La Dolce Vita*," I asked, with just a little more emotion showing than I had planned for, "where is she? I want to find her, uh, *meet* her." Fellini smiled for the first time. Like millions before me I, too, was a pilgrim in the Eternal City. I don't know how many levels my question was supposed to have, or which ones Fellini dug. Finally he shrugged his shoulders. "She's gone," he said, with a half-pouting underlip thrust up in pantomime sadness. "Like all other angels she's grown up to be a woman. That's what happens to angels." He looked at me with mock grief.

Eileen scribbled energetically. The dogs started barking again. In the fireplace of the kitchen setting a gigantic flame roared up. Technicians were spraying the exposed flesh of the extras with artificial perspiration. His co-workers call Fellini's filming "the daily miracle." They never know from day to day just what *il poeta* will expect of them. He had apparently not thought of the giant spit until the night before, and had casually told the set man to have it ready the next day. The set man told me if he had known a few days earlier he could have assembled it for a third of the cost. But Federico doesn't like to think that far ahead.

While the tumult went on, we talked a little about *Satyricon.* Like many of us, Fellini learned about Roman history not from textbooks but from third-rate movies about the justified fall of the debauched and decadent Empire. The *Satyricon,* written by Petronius Arbiter, an intimate friend of the emperor Nero, has often been read as a juicy product of Rome's dry rot. Fellini thinks not. He wants to make a movie that will show that crucial period not as a lascivious orgy and not as the lamentable decline of a once great people, but as a portrait of human beings living between the epochs. The gods of classical Rome were dead. Christianity had not yet put its stamp on the Western conscious-ness. People were taking life as it came to them, savoring what they could, reserving their ultimate commitments, coping the best they could without a firm set of accepted values and beliefs. Not only does Fellini believe we now live in a comparable time (and I agree), but I am sure he wants to stretch his own head to grasp what life might have been like, as he says, "before Christ, before the invention of conscience and guilt."

Fellini may not be entirely right about just when it was that conscience and guilt were invented. But he is right that all of us in the West, whether we think of ourselves as religious or not, are deeply touched in our very perception of reality by nearly two thousand years of more or less Christian civilization. Fellini's re-creation of the world of Nero and Petronius Arbiter has some of the same effect as his thrusting before us an unspeakably ugly man or a raving, muttering maniac. It confronts us with a reality different from our own, but one to which we are inextricably tied with the bonds of human flesh. As Fellini had told Mark Shivas of the *New York Times* about *Satyricon,* "What intrigues me is the evocation of a lost world. Not exact reconstructions. Not archeology. It is like looking at an Amazon tribe. There is no point of reference. A voyage to the unknown! . . . It must look, and the audience must see it, as though the characters speak another, completely different language, far from their understanding. . . . I just make a crazy thing about paganity."

Needless to say, filming the *Satyricon* will supply Fellini with a palette-blowing opportunity to indulge all his fondest impulses: slave girls, intrigue, excess, anomie, cruelty, dancers, and mountebanks. And serene, calmly joyous people living it all. Someone once compared Fellini to Hieronymos Bosch. I think the comparison is correct. While some interpretations of Bosch claim that his depictions of the lusts of the flesh and the evils of the world, for example in his "Garden of Earthly Delights," is eminently orthodox and was meant to warn the faithful; others say Bosch was a member of a heretical secret society that wanted man to return to such simple edenic pleasures. The truth is there is a little of each in Bosch, and in Fellini. Also, both pour on the monstrous and the grotesque first because they want to zap us into an encounter with another reality, *and* because they want us to see perverts, cripples, idiots, sadists, and weak-kneed pushovers as our brothers and sisters.

Fellini had now started directing a scene. It was all I could have hoped for: a guest at Trimalchio's feast is set upon by kitchen slaves, chased, hounded, and scalded with boiling water. While all this happens, the rest of the kitchen crew laughs uproariously. One very fat lady, stirring a huge kettle of what is supposed to be soup, shakes and quivers while she laughs. Fellini notices. He wants to shoot a close-up of the massive, rollicking, quivering human mountain, her bulbous arms and myriad cheeks shining with phony, sprayed-on sweat. Before he shoots he asks her to pull her bodice down a bit and tug her dress down over the shoulder. She gets nervous. Fellini signals to the camera crew to take a little break. Walking over he raps jovially with Maria, the fat lady, while everybody else, all two hundred of us, wait. "Maria," he says, "what a beautiful, big woman you are." Eileen is translating and filling more pages of her notebook. Maria blushes. "Maria," Fellini asks, "are you married?" "Si, Signor Fellini," she beams. "Maria, Maria," says Fellini, feigning a classical lover's pose, head tilted, arms outstretched, "how cozy and nice it must be to be in bed with you on these cold nights." Maria chuckles, and quivers. Fellini leans over and says something to her none of us can hear. Maria quivers more and laughs out loud, wipes her eyes and beams like a sunrise. Fellini slowly saunters back to his perch next to the camera. He begins again. This time Maria laughs, stands up and points to the slaves pursuing the guest, throws back her head and quivers to beat the band.

Now something goes wrong with the spit. It won't flame out. Fellini ambles back over to where Eileen and I are standing. "More brandy?" he asks. I accept. Then he starts to talk about *Mastorna,* the movie he did *not* make. *Mastorna* is Fellini's real-life *8½*. Sinking a very large pile of someone's money in elaborate preparations, including casting Marcello Mastroianni, erecting huge sets in a field outside Rome, and buying hundreds of costumes, Fellini set out to make a movie that, if the footage I saw is any clue, would have orbited from where *Juliet and the Spirits* came to rest—the outer borders of human fantasy. Fellini was obviously distressed that he could not bring himself to finish the movie. He told me that he had a whole storehouse full of costumes and that when he went in occasionally to look at them they seemed to call out to him asking why they had been abandoned. (That line sounded a little melodramatic when I heard it. Later, as I suspected, it turned out to be a line he uses in a TV short he made for CBS, but that doesn't mean it isn't true.) *Mastorna* is about a musician, a cellist who is really not at home in the "real" world. But what is the "real" world? For *Mastorna* Fellini created a set that was meant to *look* like a set. It included a huge mock-up of Cologne Cathedral and another of a TWA jetliner. Somewhere in the middle of *Mastorna,* Fellini, like Guido in *8½,* lost touch with the muse. He could not go on. So now everything hangs in limbo. After he gave up on it he first made a short piece called *Tony Dammit.* Then he started work on the *Satyricon.* Although he seemed absorbed in his present work, it struck me as strange that even in the midst of filming it he could turn to me and start talking, in such nostalgic and affectionate terms, about *Mastorna.*

Just then a technician told Fellini it would take an hour to fix the flamer on the spit. Fellini looked at his watch and suggested we go to a nearby screening room in Cinecitta and take a look at the rushes on his TV special. We did. It included some scenes from *Mastorna,* some of his exploratory sequences for *Satyricon,* and some footage he had shot while trying people out for his two most recent movies.

I found the tryout scenes the most fascinating. When Fellini is going to make a movie he puts a notice in the Rome newspaper that he will be in a downtown office trying people out. Come one, come all. And they do. Third-rate singers, birdcall specialists, strong-man acts, acrobats, great lovers—all people who want desperately to be in a Fellini movie. Fellini sits all day and watches and listens. He is not bored. These pathetic creatures pour a transfusion into his jaded veins. "They think they need me," he says in the special, "but the truth is that I need them."

The rushes are interesting but not spectacular. When the lights flash on Eileen puts her shades back on and we zip back to the set. She is ecstatic. For her it has been a good day since she's seen rushes on the special, and, as she tells me, if I had not been there, she might not have. Back at the set it is now dark and chilly. I have missed a whole afternoon session of the conference on "The Culture of Unbelief" and my conscience is prickling, but only mildly. The flaming spit is now working, but the half-naked slaves are chilly. They look odd as they shiver and stamp their feet with cold while their bodies glow with artificial perspiration. Fellini directs another part of the scene for a half an hour. By now he has donned his famous lamb's-wool jacket and his notorious broad-brimmed black hat. I stare at him in fascination. *Il poeta* is lost in creating his realer-than-real world. And the whole operation, not just what goes on in front of the camera, is part of the show. No wonder he likes an audience when he directs. He is a character in a scene in which the movie itself is only a show within a show. All that he does is autobiographical—

either what happened or what he wishes had happened or what he thinks happened or what might still happen. The line is not ·very clear. And we are all characters in the Big Movie.

Then it happened. My stream of consciousness about the way Fellini extends his movies to include the people behind the camera had led me to remember a couple of scenes in the special we had just seen. Fellini had once told an interviewer that in *Satyricon* he wanted to use Michael Pollard, the Beatles, Mae West, Danny Kaye, Jimmy Durante, and Groucho Marx. Instead he decided to use almost entirely unknown people. He really did pull employees out of the Rome stockyard and deck them out in gladiators' armor. He really did haunt the Coliseum, where many of Rome's most unsavory night people gather in the shadows. He really did dismiss Marcello Mastroianni from the part of Mastorna because he was by now too familiar a face. He did . . .

"You cold?" Fellini asked me, miming a little shiver.

"Uh, yeah," I responded eloquently. Mama mia, *what* am I doing? The world's greatest film artist stops two hundred people in the midst of the creative act to ask a stupid-assed Harvard professor if he's *cold*? It was like *coitus interruptus* and I was the interruptus. What could I do to get him back to his thing?

Fellini kept looking at me. "You want a coat?"

"Yeah, yeah," I said, "grazia."

Fellini called a flunky over and said something to him very rapidly in Italian. The assistant looked at him with surprise, paused, and then dashed for the nearest Fiat and tore off.

Eileen's pencil stopped. She took off her shades and looked me straight in the eye.

"He's getting you Mastorna's coat," she said.

The five minutes that elapsed before the Fiat came back flipped and backflipped between reality and fantasy. True, I had had three or four brandies, and on an empty stomach. True, like about a hundred million other male moviegoers I have occasionally indulged myself in a daydream of what it would be like to lead a Marcello Mastroianni life—cool, handsome, rich as sin, absolutely irresistible to women, a trifle self-indulgent, weak but likeable, etc. Also, in the unfinished movie, Mastorna-Mastroianni wore a short beard, not unlike mine. But let's face it, even with Eileen gazing at me with a new interest and the extras whispering, looking me over, nodding and shaking their heads, I am *not* Marcello. My wife thinks I am reasonably attractive and my children are impressed with my talent, but the only acting I've done since high school was as one of the murdering knights in a church-produced version of T. S. Eliot's *Murder in the Cathedral*. Even then, I nearly ruined the play one evening by lumbering in to kill Thomas Becket wearing my knight suit but having forgotten to take off my Macy's rubber overshoes. Fantasies are fine, but . . .

Fellini was not looking at me directly. He had stopped the operation and everyone was wrapped in coats, sipping coffee. He occasionally glanced my way and nodded, smiling. Suddenly a sub-extra, one of the heavy-chested little men Fellini had exhumed from the stockyard, wearing a slave's loincloth that allowed his tummy to hang out over his belt, scurried over to us. Someone had just told him what was going on and, like a late bearer of news you already had, he was telling me something in Italian. Eileen translated with great composure. No chick from the sticks she. She'd been around (she had). She was not going to twitch or wriggle or accent her tones for some cat who was being sized up by Fellini in Mastorna's coat (or just being kept warm, who the hell knows? But if he just wanted to get me warm, certainly there were coats closer than the *Mastorna* warehouse, or there were coats other than Mastorna's or . . .).

"That's the way he does it," the stockyard-man-cum-extra was piping, with Eileen translating, "that's the way he did it with me. He put that gladiator's stuff on me and gave me a sword and kept looking at me, and here I am." (Claudius Stockyardensis, however, was not now in a gladiator's suit; he was in the somewhat less resplendent garb of a pantry slave.) The coat arrived and the third assistant to the prop man held it open deferentially as I put it on. It fit. Perfectly. It was the same coat I had seen on Mas-troianni in those scenes from *Mastorna.* I buttoned it up, turned up the collar and nodded a thank-you to Fellini. He was now looking at me directly, but with no real show of interest.

Be cool, you bastard, I said to myself. I pushed my glasses up on my nose. Not that. A professorial gesture, precious, icky. What would Mastorna, the otherworldly cellist, the poet in a world of engineers, do? How should I know? I'd never even heard about Mastorna until a few hours ago. Unfair. Being sized up for a bril-liant new career in the movies without knowing what part I was trying out for. My worst, recurrent, accomplishment-oriented nightmare coming true. But what the hell, even if he offered it to me (offered *what,* he's not even making the damn movie! Not now he's not, but someday he will), I couldn't, wouldn't, shouldn't take it. Seize hold of yourself. A theologian, author of a best-selling theological book, a full professor at Harvard. Heed not the siren voice of *il poeta.* Federico, you're luring me into your game, the cosmic conspiracy of the put-on artist and the put-upon, the quiet joust of mutual exploitation and charlatanry that makes the world go around. "All Fellini's actors start out that way," someone was saying to me. "It's all a shellgame and then, click, you're in a movie." Or maybe you're on the way home. "I need them more than they need me."

At 10:00 I had been there for eight hours and I was hungry. Eileen had invited me to a dinner with some people from Fellini's entourage at the home of a friend. I said good-bye to *il poeta,* thanked him for the coat, and offered to give it back. He waved it away, kissed Eileen, and told me I could give it to her to return the next day. I started to tell Fellini I had enjoyed the day, but he wasn't listening. He was looking at me, but he was not listen-ing. We left.

In the quiet of my Boston study I am sure now it was all a perfectly understandable thing. Eileen told me, as did the script girl, that they had never seen Fellini put Mastorna's coat on any-one else. Whether he has done it since I don't know. I guess I really don't want to know.

## The Purpose of the Grotesque in Fellini's Films

From his earliest years Fellini has nursed an obsessive fascination with con men and put-on artists. Sometimes he seems hard on them, as he does in *Il Bidone*. Sometimes he seems neutral, as with the hypnotist in *Cabiria*. As he matured, Fellini took the impostor, the play-actor, as his parable of life itself. Zampano tricks people into thinking he is really breaking the chains around his chest. But Il Matto, the clown, who also appears in *La Strada*, is the vehicle of grace for Gelsomina. A prankster, a rogue, a death-defying tightrope walker—he cannot take life fully seriously. But he saves Gelsomina from despair. In *8½* Guido is constantly accompanied by an articulate intellectual who analyzes and reanalyzes his scripts and his ideas from a perfectly reasonable, intelligent point of view. He congratulates Guido when he decides to give up. But just then an aging charlatan-magician whom Guido had met at the spa sticks his head in his car and asks him if it isn't time to get going. Guido agrees. Out come the people who have bugged, bothered, and beset Guido throughout the movie. They form a huge circle and dance around to the music of the circus band. The deceiver has his hollow wand on a truth that is more profound than the reasonable man knows of.

Maybe Fellini was putting me on. Maybe he was playing around with the dream of finding a new Mastorna. Maybe he just wanted to keep me from catching cold. I kept the coat for three days. When I dropped it at Eileen's office she wasn't there. She had left a message that Fellini was filming that afternoon at the beach (where some of the scenes from *Juliet* had been shot) and wanted to see me again, maybe have lunch. I left the coat and took the taxi to the airport. Getting on the plane I wore my new, wrap-around Italian shades. I sipped a delicious martini. When the stewardess asked me if I'd like my dinner, I looked up at her over my shades and gave her a very knowing, Mastroianni smile. Weak, overpowered creature. How could she do anything but curl up in the empty seat beside me and stroke my head during the long flight ahead?

"Yeah," I said, quietly but very sexily.

She stopped smiling and put the dinner down on my tray.

105

Rome, Italy, sank out of sight as the plane continued to climb. Pretty soon I fell asleep and didn't wake up until the wheels of the jet touched down in New York. The stewardess was nowhere to be seen. After clearing customs I drank a very large cup of very black coffee before catching the shuttle back to Boston.

# 8

# Counterrevolution
# in the Movies

William F. Lynch

In the general game of countermovements that goes on in modern cinema, I would like to say a word about a counterrevolution against the underground revolution. True, it is something of a disadvantage nowadays to be caught aboveground. Nevertheless, I wish now, in the terrible daylight, to speak in behalf of words and ideas in modern cinema, to pronounce in praise and appraisal of speech and thought in the movies. To do so, surely, makes me no worse than those people who, not knowing what a picture is all about, praise the photography. And whatever the faults of my counterrevolution, they are nothing compared to those who would reduce James Joyce to visuality.

First, a few words about words. Let me begin by saying that I believe them to be very good things; they have their place, and they deserve better treatment from most people. And they should not be so ignored by so many artists, especially by those who work in films. A few of my own artist friends (who should know better) have been telling me over the years that there are people who think in terms of things-and-images and people who think in words. This was, unfortunately, one of the general impressions that had spread about widely. One of the results of this kind of dichotomy was that the life of words was surrendered to the wrong people and was often given up by the wrong people. They were the kind of people who were capable of separating words from images. They tended to divide the world into imagination and sensibility on the one side and a something called thought and thinking on the other, though both sides really knew that *they* were right and they were the thinkers. My own opinion is that it was words (and "ideas") that suffered most from the division and the battle. They lost a half of their life as a result of their separation from the imagination. I leave it to the historians to tell us how much of their true souls philosophy and theology lost in this sequel. My own interest will be in the specific direction of the cinema and the form in which the battle frequently emerges there between image and word. For I think the assumption of many people is that this new visual-aural medium is most authentic (if I may use that blessed word once and nevermore) when it is most visual and least so where it is also composed of words, words, words (or of the equally unfortunate entities called ideas).

## Out of Touch with Existence

Let me hypothesize in a few directions. One of the reasons for the struggle between words and images may be that we have decided that our modern intellectual situation has been fundamentally schizophrenic, that a good deal of the life of the intelligence has been out of touch with existence, and that images are a better way than words to recontact existence. I think that is why we want pure Happenings. My first hypothesis is that we want them because we do not have them. That is why some people agree to look at hour-long simple images in the new-new *vogue*. Because maybe the thing is not really there. That is why it was such a fortunate moment for Susan Sontag to come along with her book *Against Interpretation*. And she picked the right moment to proclaim that "whatever it may have been in the past, the idea of content is today mainly a hindrance, a nuisance, a subtle or not so subtle philistinism." [1] It was a propitious moment, a moment that was hungry for the slightest taste of reality and that was impatient with anything that tasted of remoteness from experience, of anything that smacked of interpretation, of anything that, in my language, tasted of words, words, words. Let us make no mistake about it: *Against Interpretation* was published at a full tide of a movement against interpretation, against content, against words, against ideas. Many were so starved that they could not abide any interpretation. Therefore, she could proclaim: "The world, our world, is depleted, impoverished enough. Away with all duplicates of it, until we again experience more immediately what we have." [2] Miss Sontag is not against words, as many people are, but she seems to me, with her plea for immediacy of experience, to put her finger on one of the root reasons that words have fallen into disrepute in certain areas of our culture. These areas are committed to the need and primacy of immediate experience and I am myself hypothesizing that the main reason for this commitment is the out-of-touchness of many with existence. And when we are out of touch, we will resort to violence to restore contact.

Let me be as clear as possible in this matter, even syllogistically clear. If we were to look at the old syllogism (if there is a finite, there is an infinite; but there is a finite; therefore, there is an infinite), then the real trouble may very well be not with the major premise or the conclusion, but with the minor premise: Is there really a finite, are things really there; or have words, art forms, our structures, and our psychologistic life destroyed them? People try to convince themselves that their problem is God; but the problem is actually one step nearer than that. Miss Sontag herself is not far from saying this, in such sentences as: "The new formalism of the French novels and films is . . . a dedicated agnosticism about reality itself." [3] But she makes a mistake when she cites Antonioni's *L'Avventura* as an example of a good film with "a directness that entirely frees us from the itch to interpret." [4] For surely *L'Avventura* is all about a lack of directness in experience, whether with people or things, and is itself an enormous interpretation. Again the fact is that there is so much talk about experience because there is so little of it. Such separation from experience is inevitably accompanied by an absence of the feelings and relations that normally attach themselves to finite existence, and the results, obviously, can be very painful.

## William F. Lynch

It is by now a cliché to note the absence of real verbal relationships in Antonioni's films, but what is not so usually pointed out is his metaphorical transfer of this death of words to external objects. Neither do they talk to each other, in the sense that often there is neither sequence nor relationship in the objects that catch the eye of the camera. And objects are not talking to each other because this is the way the camera is talking to itself, in patches and pieces, in thoughts that occur but do not come together in paragraphs, whether the paragraphs be visual or vocal. Monica Vitti is distracted even from the intensity of a sexual incident. This is also true of what we can call the incident and episode quality of so much of Antonioni's work; this is not formalistic exploration at all but a formal declaration of content, to the effect that incident does not speak to incident, that nothing is related to nothing. But let me correct the end clause of my own last sentence. Antonioni is not making a philosophical remark that no object or incident connects with any other, or speech with speech. He is analyzing the passivity of the camera, and the camera is the mind and eye of his people. The camera is listless; it is dead; it is condemning itself.

If such a degree of alienation really exists (I think that our love of it is on the way out), things would be bad enough. But my real concern is to say that it would be even worse to decide and declare that words themselves are among our chief villains as alienators from existence and that we must not hope for anything much from words as we thrash about for a new contact with existence through images and objects. However, we shall see that there is not only a movement away from words, for the reasons suggested, but there is also, happily, a countermovement toward words and "ideas" as means of contacting existence.

### Breaking Out of the Private Trap

It is almost unnecessary to indicate how much of modern cinema is a description of our failure or inability to make this contact. One special quality of some of these descriptions is the effective way in which they picture what we might call *the private*

110

(in the sense of the self-enclosed) as desperate attempts at passage into reality. There *has been* a separation from public reality. It is not only that in Bergman and Antonioni we have desperate attempts of people to make this passage and contact, but the attempts are clearly set off from any communication with the rest of the world. So much is this true in *Silence* that its sexuality is largely incestuous; there are only a few flashes of the existence of an outside world, and the language of that world is foreign and unintelligible. What is particularly beautiful about its ending is that the woman and boy in the train finally have set to the business of learning the language of the world with which they are surrounded. (This is the new demand being made on the novelist, that he learn the language of the world.) As any nonlinguistic tourist knows, there is nothing as self-enclosing, and as defeating of experience, as an ignorance of the language of a country. It seems to me, therefore, that in *Silence* language is representative of the passage from private to public reality.

And it may very well be that, after a long period of self-enclosure, we are now entering the first phases of a bitter and powerful attack on the private and the intense private experience as paths to anything much. The satire is growing. Fellini's *Juliet of the Spirits* is a satirical analysis of the history of private fantasy in our long attempt to form an adequate public image of woman. *The Knack* does just as good a job as satire on adolescent and private fantasy in sexuality. Resnais's very recent *La Guerre est Finie* is a critical analysis of the private language dream in the kind of revolutionary who should, above all others, be inserted into the public reality but who, instead, is playing like a child at a game of unreal counters where the past has never changed into the present and the past is the only reality. These, I am sure, are only a few examples of a counterrevolution that has set in in the name of what we can call public reality and public speech.

I am hopeful that we are moving toward the restoration of what I like to call the public imagination. And with this movement a number of parallel things are occurring. The *love* and affection for alienation, the fascination for the thing, is beginning to ebb. It is possible that the intellectuals may be and have been much more the alienated ones in a wasteland than Mr. Sweeney and Tom, Dick, and Harry, who seem not as unhappy as T. S. Eliot thought. And there is a new demand in the air that the imagination give up its self-enclosed life, that it should be filled with two things as first acts of its work: concern and knowledge.

In this essay, therefore, I suggest that there are two movements going on, counter to each other and to some extent causing each other by counteraction. I could summarize each quickly in the following way:

(1) Movement number one is toward immediate, private, and wordless experience. Its appearance is inevitable in a culture where public experience tends to run short. It is inevitable that it should deliberately fragment experiences, that it should be against interpretation, and that it should have, if not a bias, at least a disinclination away from words and ideas. There is an increasing suspicion abroad that it has been enjoying its alienation.

(2) The second and opposite movement, and the one in which I am cinematically interested at the moment, can in summary be called a movement of images in the codirection of words and ideas. It is not only a countermovement to "against interpretation"; it not only interprets; it moves, in fact, right up into the explicit and stylized forms of the old morality and mystery plays. And this includes the works of some of the best directors of our day. It is daring enough to play around with all kinds of generalizations. And it is not afraid to use words and speech in the most direct, simple, and general way.

I think that the new materials may for two reasons turn out to be very important. One reason I have already given: words and ideas have been given a hard time; they had been pushed into a polarized state, devoid of contact with images and things. They needed to be allowed to reenter the world and to reestablish their relation to things and their own power as a human art. The second reason for the importance of this phenomenon is that apparently it is so extremely natural. People like words and they like ideas. And they like fine words and big ideas. Of course they are often fooled, or drawn by the phony in words and ideas, but no more often than are the intellectuals by the world of pure things and the purely visual.

First I go back to words and film. One of my own central feelings is expressed also by Pauline Kael who has stressed that talking pictures must indeed pay attention to speech with all of its powers and splendors and problems, for speech does retain its ability to move us through the register of emotions.[5] It is possible that we have become afraid of great speech and have decided we are unworthy to use it.

My second central feeling is that there should be no single law about their usage in film, except the very flexible one that the thing come off well.

We should not start with the supposition, as many do, that contemporary film is fundamentally a visual art, to which words may be added. We should not even decide that if in a film something can be expressed visually then it should not be expressed by sound or speech. Alfred Hitchcock tells us that image is the heart of the matter and sound is only a supplement.

Another apparently attractive law that should be ruled out is that of economy in the use of words. It is better to follow the more flexible direction of Carl Dreyer who stressed that the matter of primary importance was that what appears on the screen be interesting and that the question of dominance of text or image be subordinate to the evocation of interest. Limiting a film within the confines of any set of rules can limit the ability of the film to arouse interest.

But then even Dreyer, in the next breath, insists that the trial techniques of *The Passion of Joan of Arc* demanded a synchronization of, an equation between, speech and close-up. It is hard to see why a dozen other alternatives could not have been chosen from, but this was a case where rigidity of decisions was most fortunate and led to a masterpiece of sculptured faces that film history would be the poorer without. And it is clear that it was a splendid reality, the face of Miss Falconetti, that had more to do with the particular alternative chosen than all the court procedures in the world. It is not every face we would wish to watch as it formed words according to the natural and realistic norm that speech should synchronize with the movements of the lips.

It is in fact interesting to note that as far back as 1930, Eisenstein, Pudovkin, and Alexandrov were saying the contrary and were pleading for a nonrealistic asynchronism between images and words: "Only the method of using sound in counterpoint with the visuals offers new possibilities for developing and perfecting the art of montage. Experiment with sound should be concentrated on using asynchronism between sound and visuals. This approach will lead in time to the creation of a new orchestral counterpoint of visual and sound images." [6]

But surely asynchronism and counterpoint should be determined by idea, by what you want to say. The medium of asynchronism should be determined by the message. Resnais is one of a number of directors who is interested in the nature of reality and the reality and irreality of the past. Put very simplistically, this is what is on his mind and it is, therefore, altogether natural that he use certain nonnatural forms of asynchronism in the word-image process. Thus, in the recent *La Guerre est Finie* he has Yves Montand as a revolutionary on the run moving through a veritable sea of verbal directives and comments that exist in the air as an atmosphere of intrigue. Go here. Go there. See him. See her. This will lead in a chain to that, and that to this. The words come from no lips but form an atmosphere and a life. They describe a kind of child's game which is being played, but here are grown-up men taking it very seriously, no longer able to distinguish between reality and dream. And where is reality in the picture? That is the question. For a time it is in Montand, with his ever so strong and intelligent look and walk as he listens to the voices. For a time he is the foil who judges the asynchronistic and counterpointed voices. He judges the young and their voices, with their foolish revolutionary dreams. And he judges the formalist speeches of his superiors, who are giving rote reactions, rooted in the past, to the impossibilities of the present. There is a formalism and a roteness in *their* speeches which judges their every word as a mechanical voice from the past, out of touch with that reality which is rooted in his strong, omnipotent, all-seeing eyes. But Montand, too, will yield to the dream and the game. He will judge it and play with it. He is, we suddenly realize, both Sancho Panza and Don Quixote. But he remains beyond final judgment in the picture—because he remains judge, strong man, actualist, dreamer, cowboy, good guy, bad guy, dream, reality, everything. And the secret of his specious strength is his silence. Everybody else speaks and is judged by his words. But the camera will not give the hero away. It will not let him talk.

The counterpoint, then, is between the voices of the past and the central judging eyes of the present revolutionary. The past is judged to be both dead and beautiful. Nevertheless, the past, by words, is solidly inserted into the present, corrupting it, destroying it, filling it with lies, and making it impossible that anyone see what is in front of him. And the visual, silent hero succumbs to the voices.

The result of this interplay of words and images in *La Guerre est Finie* must, I think, be called successful, as the earlier explorations into counterpuntal speech and images by Resnais in *Hiroshima Mon Amour* and *Last Year at Marienbad* must be called essentially artificial. In these other two cases Resnais, perhaps dreaming of the long-ago victories of French symbolism, came through with hundreds of unreal words spoken by unreal men and women before a camera that dare not judge the general phoniness. The thing comes off better in *La Guerre est Finie* because the words come not out of Mallarme but out of ordinary people about to throw a bomb that probably will not work.

There can be as many counterpointings of speech and imagery, as much asynchronism between the two, as there are things and messages to be said in these ways about reality. In a recent English spy thriller, *The Deadly Affair,* the words of Marlow describing the murder of Edward II are being heard on a stage while a modern spy murder is taking place in the body of the auditorium, so that it is the voice of the past which is describing

115

the action of the present. And the message is that the real play is in the auditorium. But it is easy to forget that this new cinematic use of a play within a play was probably borrowed from Shakespeare, and that we shall not have arrived at a use of it in contemporary terms (which likes to play with the checkerboard of the question, Where is reality?) until we are given an example of a play within a play within a play within a play. And I promise you that I will give it.

What we must obviously be interested in is the creative relationship between sounds and images. A single sound in *La Strada,* the sound of the haunting tune brought back from the past at the end of the picture, is enough to restore every image of the past in the picture and to drive mad the mind of man. In *Riffi* and *Topkapi* the fear of a possible sound breaking in on silence-at-all-costs can be overwhelming, and the images of the consequence of sound are always there as background and atmosphere. The words that are about to come out of a victrola record and devastate a human being at the end of Graham Greene's *Brighton Rock* fill one with a horror that much resembles the final word of truth from the shepherd that is about to strike the ears of Oedipus. What is created in both cases by the very possibility of speech is the image of a dreadful chasm the consciousness is about to cross, and a brink.

"O God, I am on the brink of frightful speech."

"And I of frightful hearing. . . ."[7]

The whole play demands this word. And this word is the central image of the play. And so with the picture.

In *A Man for All Seasons* all the language must be examined with a microscope to make sure it is maintaining silence and not using speech about the one thing that matters. The audience is drawn into the general legal concern for the words; it is concerned that they be silent words at all costs, because they know that one slip from the mouth and the whole head will slip off the neck of Thomas More. The words that conjure the headless image finally do come out, but they come from the mouth of a venal perjurer, not from Thomas More. And as the perjurer, who has as his reward the revenue office of Wales, passes out of the court, More says to him: "Richard, you should not so give up your soul for the whole world. But for Wales! . . ." For Wales! "Oh, the pity of it," says More, and the words conjure up the faces of all the sad, smiling Welshmen as they receive this last message from Thomas. And I do not doubt that there is a double take here, comically, to the present men of Wales, for Paul Scofield himself is from there.

### Reverse of Maxims

Part of what I am saying is the reverse of the usual maxim that if a thing can be said visually in film then let it not be said in words. I am saying that, as in life itself, there should also be a film maxim: Where one word can create so many images, why ask the camera to do it? But, again, there are no laws. The commonplace Don Juan in *Alfie* talks a lot, and he talks to his audience, because he is very conscious of his own silliness and of our appraisal and must be constantly explaining himself. *His* talk is an attempt to justify an image that cannot stand on its own two feet.

That there is much talk and many words in these pictures, as well as in *Who's Afraid of Virginia Woolf,* only becomes a critical remark when there is some missing of the point. The quantity and the vigor of the words in *Virginia Woolf* are, on the first surface, ordinary human words that say something. On the second level they turn out to be words describing games being played at, unrealities, fictions. On the third and final take they have inflexibly human rules behind them and are the only forms of salvation and contact, cruel though they be, between George and Martha. In this particular case it *happens* to be words that contribute new dimensions to our separations and that make this picture, it seems to me, a more human and profound analysis of silence and speech than the more posed and more visual work of Antonioni. Silence, therefore, is no sign of depth or superiority. Nor is speech, for that matter, if we remember the pretentious speech of *Last Year in Marienbad.* There are no laws.

117

I was about to make the general suggestion that the contemporary cinema needs to be more daring in the use of words—I mean words, not daring words, for that is not the problem—when I was able to see *Ulysses* and to see that here it has been done. I had thought that there should be no a priori limitation of any kind in the screen use of words: Why could we not in some cases have nothing but words and beautiful print and read together, by the hundreds and thousands? Why should reading always be a private act? Why could not the printed word sometimes be the center and once again breathe forth miniature images? Of course *Ulysses* does none of these extreme things, but it is one of our greatest cinematic ventures yet in the great use of words. (Its trouble will come later when it reappears in the hands of the large theater chains and the advertisers.) In it the images move through a haunting text of words which they fight hard to measure up to, and the words are the life of the human mind meditating on the inner and outer reality of Man and Woman. This is the omnipresent image, never seen, created by the words: the thinking, brooding mind and fantasy of man. And speech is at its fullest, allowed to float in the air. Let me turn my own text here from words to the life of ideas and the life of the mind.

What I am interested in right now is the use of highly general and interpretative words in cinema, and their relation to images. To explain this interest I repeat my early remarks on the unhappy dichotomy we had tended to create between a thing and image world on the one hand and pure words and "ideas" on the other. Now the question can be asked: Is it possible there will be fruitful consequences from a rebinding of these two worlds in contemporary cinema? Reflective thinking, especially in theology and religion, has suffered so much through these separations from the imagination and the images of the artist.

It will probably surprise most people how much and how often the contemporary film falls into a broad reflective style in dealing with what we have the habit of calling "ideas," and in doing what we have habitually called "thinking." So I am not pleading for a development in this direction, but rather pointing to its existence as one of the strong habits of our film artists. I take no thought of the large stream of pictures drawn from biblical and formally spiritual traditions when I repeat, for the sake of sharpening my point, that a good many films are veering toward the general forms, feelings, and style of medieval morality plays. The cinema has become an explorer not only of words but of ideas as well, in forms that are often deliberately simple and naive. And both artists and audiences seem to be enjoying the new adventures to an uncalculated degree.

A number of pictures come close to being visual-oral essays on metaphysics, with additions in technique that could well have been drawn from Russian roulette and the old army game. What is reality, and where is it? Now you see, now you don't. It may hit you when you are not expecting it. We don't have it, and are far away from it. Bergman's *The Magician* is an orchestration of the many forms of our understanding of what reality is, and where. In it there is camera reality, actor's reality, magician's reality, reality as seen by a wife doing a job on her police inspector husband, adolescent reality, reality under hypnosis that conforms to another mind, the reality of the scientist who is frightened by the reality of the magician. The latter turns out to be the doing of a job and another good show, to the doing of which he is summoned by the king; and so the picture ends, with a proud human flourish around so big a theme.

Antonioni's *Blow-up* is full of created events and happenings; the one real event, the only reality of the picture, a murder, becomes ultimately lost to consciousness as the welter and intensity of pseudo-events and posed emotions overwhelm the mind. At the end all the actors are watching a tennis match with absolute commitment, and the ball goes back and forth, the dedicated heads with it. They are watching a ball that is not there. And the one thing that is truly there is not there.

What reality do other people have, in the midst of all our preoccupying thoughts? Are they really there? Can we break through to them? Are objects as separated from each other as people from people? Are fidelity and love possible human virtues? These are other huge and generalizing questions of Antonioni in *L'Avven-*

*tura, The Night, Eclipse.* I wonder how these people and these words would sound if they spoke aloud the great generalities of these images. I am not a cynic in these matters. I think it would come off very well.

The spy story is not content to be a spy story anymore but is beginning, in its own style, to enunciate on the large human plane. It is no longer a matter of the good guys versus the bad guys, or us natives against them foreigners; there begin to be no good guys anymore. Now all is betrayal, and no one can be trusted, and the human heart is a treacherous thing, always ready to betray not only others but itself most of all. This is the fundamental atmosphere of *The Spy Who Came in from the Cold* and *The Deadly Affair.* In them we are talking about the awful beast called Human Nature.

Or how could Everyman be more at the center of the cinematic stage than he is in such pictures as *Woman in the Dunes* or *Rashomon.* The former is a parable about the basic structures of human existence as struggle with the universe, the forging of a clearing in the endless dark and the endless sand, the discovery of the flesh, the birth of a child, the warfare between good and evil, the faint glimmer of a farther shore. *Rashomon* becomes a brooding lament over the conflict of lie with lie as every human heart paints reality with its own wishes and purposes. Another Japanese picture, *Ikiru,* seems very clearly to be a redoing of *Everyman,* with its announcement of death, the abandonment by friends, and the triumphant resort to good deeds.

### Revolt against the Wasteland

All these pictures can be called morality plays with almost as much accuracy as such old English plays as the "Pater Noster" play of York, *The Pride of Life, The Castle of Perseverance, The Nature of the Four Elements,* and the great document of *Everyman* itself. We are in the midst of a charming and not quite explainable movement toward the human, the general, the didactic.

But, alas, the issue is often sadly reversed from that of the medieval situation. On the morality stage the play usually took the form of a contest for the soul of a representative of the whole human race, and the chief actor made it; he was saved! Now the characters don't seem to be making it, and we are more often dealing with the dread eventuality of the loss of the soul, to the extent that "the loss of the self" has become a cliché. Sometimes· the loss of the soul and its abandonment to someone else is done handsomely and powerfully, as in *The Servant.* Sometimes the damnation, abandonment, and takeover has neither style, quality, sense, nor competence, and is no credit to heaven or hell, as in *Persona,* a picture which temporarily dims the Bergman luster. But there is the beginning of a revolt in the air against the general wasteland and be-damned concept of our reality, and a revolt against those people at cocktail parties who go around asking, "Do you really know who you are? Are you really saved?" Fear not, there will always be a priesthood, and this is the latest, with sophisticated damnation in its not so steady hand. I wish there were more on the saved side in their theology. But most of us, in the new reckoning, are damned, irrevocably.

Next: if you want commentaries on the universal decadence and boredom of life, there they are—to the point of growing boredom but still a testament to the strange attraction of generality—in *La Dolce Vita, This Sporting Life, The Easy Life,* and *Darling.* The medieval vices are rearing their ugly heads again.

I have the impression that, where it is at all well done, film audiences are easily and deeply fascinated by the raising of general questions about life. And we are so deeply immersed in our theories of the concrete nature of vision in art and literature that we forget this other fascination for parable, legend, and generality, and find it hard to explain. T. S. Eliot was caught by the ideal beauty of *Everyman.* A modern audience is quite caught by the poignant images and questions about death in *The Seventh Seal.* I am not pretending to give an explanation. I am only stating what seems an audience fact.

Part of the continuing fascination of *La Strada* lies not only in the emergence of the childlike soul and face of the girl but also in the childlike emergence of the simple theme (we say that art

121

should not have a theme, but we often bow to its charm). The theme here is that even a little stone has its vocation in the universe; it is a wonderful thing, and a relief, that this girl has one too; and a tragedy when she loses it.

Then there are the growing number of studies in different forms of fantasy versus reality, each approaching the form of a general essay on the subject. I have noted that *Juliet of the Spirits* is largely a review of the history of human fantasy about woman; *The Knack* is an essay on adolescent fantasy within the order of sexuality. And way back, twenty years ago, one remembers that magnificent commentary on death and the love of money, stolen out of *The Pardoner's Tale* by John Huston, in *The Treasure of the Sierra Madre.* How beautiful a combination of legend and morality play it was!

Possibly I am going too far afield, but not too much, when I think, in the same breath of fantasy, about such clear-lined, clear-limned pictures as *The Bridge on the River Kwai* and *Lawrence of Arabia.* Is part of the great popular success of both due to a deep and powerful fundamental clarity of line and of the theme that any form of absoluteness in the rigid and driving human will is a threat to man and is bound to blow up the picture and the man at the end? Actually the leads in both pictures, under the weight of their own single-minded ideas, do blow up or fall apart.

### Danger! Men Thinking

Thus, cinematic words and ideas are very much in our midst. Clearly there is more than one movement in contemporary films. Clearly there are many who are not altogether accepting the dicta of the opposite school to the effect that words and ideas are the great enemy. They had been told by one contemporary writer that they should "deny the very existence of mind." Another had told them that art must display "nothing from life, no knowledge of its affairs, no familiarity with its emotions." How often had they been told that they must not "know" anything. And D. H. Lawrence had attacked the act of cognition itself as our most fundamental act of disobedience against God and an attack on the divine in man. But despite all this and a thousand more things like it, there is this countermovement of words and ideas. And it is highly probable that we have passed over a divide in these many areas. I would ask the scholars of the contemporary theater if something revolutionary in the direction of that vulgar thing called thinking is not occurring on the stage as well. And I have mentioned the new demand on the novelist that he *know* a good deal as the first act of his imagination.

Then, and finally, there is *The Persecution and Assassination of Jean-Paul Marat as Performed by the Inmates of the Asylum of Charenton under the Direction of the Marquis de Sade.* Here it is the horror picture or play that right before our unseeing eyes has turned speechifier, theorist, metaphysical, morality; and reality within fantasy within reality within fantasy; and play within play within play within play. Once, when visiting a library, I saw a sign placed on the table by a juvenile delinquent which read: DANGER, MEN WORKING. Now when I come out of these detective and spy and horror pictures I share his feelings and I have the wish to put up a neon sign saying: DANGER, MEN THINKING.

In *Marat-Sade* the audience has come to see a play (and now a film). But they will not watch people doing and saying things. The people on the stage are themselves putting on a play. And because the actors are madmen they cannot help but break away again and again from their director and give their own version of the play, and their own reactions, thus establishing a play within a play within a play. In order to calm both the actors and the audience they are both advised that the actions being presented happened long ago and are an unreality. But the real thing that is thus said, behind sarcasm and irony, is that the realities of present-day history are far worse. By a fourth maneuver, therefore, it is now established that all previous plays are aiming at the real play in the audience. The real assassinations, the real revolution, the real madness, the real demagogues, are in the audience. And what is that occurring on the stage? It is real feeling erupting again and again, and not mere playacting. That is a real knife that is in the hands of the actress—it is better for her fellow actor not to trust that knife—and at the end the revolution that is being acted out upon the stage becomes a real revolution, a real and terrifying bedlam. The audience has become reality. Now the play becomes it.

The final play, however, is surely going on in the playwright's mind. I cannot quite tell what that play is. It is the play which says all these things and produces all the other plays. It is the central play which is doing all the manipulating and all the thinking. And I repeat my plea that we denominate it as such, that is to say, as thinking, and hold it to the responsibilities and the consequences of that noble vocation of human thought and judgment—which leads me to the picture and the play I had almost forgotten, the real stage where all other plays and plots take place, the stage of our own minds. For it is we who cannot be absolved from making the final judgments and writing the final script. Like the inmates of Charenton we are always putting on our own plays. We too shall yield to the control of no one else, especially if we have been warned by the sign, DANGER, MEN THINKING. We can at least be as sensible as the inmates of the insane asylum who keep reacting and judging. We must not yield to the theory of the absolute art object. We must, with sense, interpret at any cost.

All kinds of final questions crowd in upon the mind as I bring these reflections toward an end.

What is the possible range of such work in ideas in the cinema? What are the virtues and limitations of competent analyses and didacticism in movie images? We cannot say that such matters are forbidden to art and the artists because art and the artists are already practicing these things on us. And they cannot play it both ways by hiding behind the name of art and saying that art is not vulnerable to our questions. Certainly this is one of the weaknesses I should like to point out as momentarily present in this new kind of work, that it is often too brilliant, that in much of it there is too much gimmickry of the intellectual life, that there are too many mirror tricks reflecting fantasy into reality and reality into fantasy and plays into plays into plays. The difficulty about many of these discussions of reality is their own aura of unreality. They tend, many of them, to fall into the new net of pure inwardness and nonrelation to reality or commitment that Philip Rieff has summarized in his new book, *The Triumph of the Therapeutic*. It is as though it is being said to us, as it is said to the mad inmates of Charenton, that we must not really get excited about these questions of freedom, anger, injustice, revolution, that it is only an art object and must not be taken seriously.

It is because I think that much serious work can be done in this direction that I think we ought to call the artist thinker and label these pictures as serious and that we ought to hand out that sign, DANGER, MEN THINKING. And I think that every resource of the cinema—images, words, ideas—deserves development; and that every manner of talent—the painter, the poet, the philosopher —should be invited in.

I mean this as a solemn warning that the medium is thinking. We ought to know what we are paying more and more money for. There ought to be a label.

## NOTES

1. Susan Sontag, *Against Interpretation and Other Essays* (New York: Farrar, Strauss & Giroux, 1966), p. 11.

2. Ibid., p. 7.

3. Ibid., p. 14.

4. Ibid., p. 18.

5. See Pauline Kael, "Are the Movies Going to Pieces?" *Atlantic Monthly*, December 1964, pp. 61-66.

6. Sergei Eisenstein, *Film Form* (Cleveland: World Publishing Co., 1968), p. 258.

7. *Oedipus Rex*, in David Grene and Richmond Lattimore, eds., *Sophocles I* (Chicago: University of Chicago Press, 1954), line 1112.

# 9

# Film, Reality, and Religion

Robert W. Wagner

To the man who knows nothing, mountains are mountains,
waters are waters, and trees are trees.
But when he has studied and knows a little, mountains
are no longer mountains,
water is no longer water, and trees are no longer trees.
But when he has thoroughly understood,
mountains are once again mountains,
waters are waters, and trees are trees.
— *Ancient Zen Buddhist philosophy*

Cinema today, more than ever before in its history, is distinguished by "moving images" propelled more by the force of relevant ideas than by a sprocket drive; produced more through "persistence of visionaries" than by persistence of vision. It is a time of The Film: a time for new film-makers and new audiences, when young people in particular seem to find in this curiously wrought medium a unique, and perhaps the only valid, means of expression in a confused and ambiguous world, short of mass demonstration or individual withdrawal. Film and television imagery seems to offer a kind of organizational and re-creative refuge in a flood of empty verbalisms and senseless realia.

It is not surprising, therefore, that the educator and the theologian begin to give serious attention to this medium, though, except for a few voices crying in the wilderness, such attention

comes a little late. It seems that otherwise knowledgeable men
had forgotten that the moving image, with its beginning in symbolism and myth, mysticism and magic, was originally more the
concern of artists, preachers, and teachers than of technologists,
inventors, and showmen. The wall paintings seen by the light of
flickering torches in the ceremonial caves of Altamira and Lascaux
were part of this prehistory of film, along with the work of
Athanasius Kircher, the Jesuit priest and teacher who presented
the first "magic lantern" show to a group of ecclesiastics in the
Collegio Romano sometime in 1644 or 1645.

Remember, too, that the work of the ancient artist who created
the image of the running boar in the cave at Altamira was forgotten for more than ten thousand years; Kircher was accused
of practicing "black art" and advised by his critics to stick to his
task of teaching mathematics; and when François Arago, in 1839,
first publicly described Daguerre's method of making images "by
the action of solar rays," the Leipzig *Anzeiger* immediately attacked what was soon to be called the process of photography as
"sacrilegious."

The use of religious terms and references in film comment today
is more than a curious coincidence in the light of this background.
Stanley Kauffmann refers to the fervor of followers of the underground film as "apostolic."[1] Kracauer writes about the "redemption" of reality and, in turn, is scored by critic Pauline Kael as
being a "religious zealot."[2] Henry Miller once wrote that "the
newsreel is the eye of God; the animated cartoon is the soul
tossing in its anguish."[3] Jean Renoir satirized the studio camera
as a kind of god, "fixed on its tripod or crane, which is just like
a heathen altar; and about it are the high priests—the director,
cameraman, assistants—who bring victims before the camera like
burnt offerings."[4]

The image, and especially the photographic image, is still invested with mysticism and regarded with concern. From the
"I.D." card with its stark, self-conscious image proving *who* we
are, to the snapshot, caught in an unguarded but decisive moment,
that tells something of *what* we are, the fact that some part of our

living being can be captured and held *in situ* arouses a kind of primordial reaction. In contemporary man it may take the form of an uneasy feeling that he increasingly is being brought under the surveillance of the camera eye in matters such as check-cashing, and under its influence every time he turns on a television set. Among the simple peoples of the world, as in the case of many Indians in the *altiplano* of South America, there is a widespread belief that part of the spirit is taken away with the photograph and is in the possession of the ubiquitous tourist-photographer whom they try, usually unsuccessfully, to avoid.

The power of the recorded image and the fear with which it was held is, of course, also reflected in both the Hebraic tradition where no material image of Yahweh was permitted, and in the tradition of Islam where the figure of the Prophet, or his family, may not be portrayed on the screen, although "symbolic" figures are allowed.[5]

The impossibility of visualizing the Great Abstraction or the Ultimate Truth in film form is a preoccupation with certain humanists and, indeed, with those in film circles. Critic Richard Dyer MacCann is only half correct when he says: "There is no such thing as religion on film; there can only be a film about human behavior as it responds to religious feeling or understanding. The basis of film is its visibility, its reproduction of a material image. Religion is concerned with that which is invisible."[6]

He is right if by a "religious film" we mean the vacuous attempts at what has been called the "bathrobe-and-beard" school of film-making, or the moralizing drawing-room drama. He is also wrong unless religious thought is so invisible that it can never be expressed in human actions, whereupon its relevance may well be questioned as it is today. Film, like the human spirit, "moves" in mysterious ways, and as this still-young medium matures it continues to expand our horizons not only beyond the limited range of our seeing and hearing, but also beyond our pretheories of film. What Walter Lippmann once wrote of the political world might also be applied to other areas of human thought, including religion:

The world we have to deal with politically is out of reach, out of sight, out of mind. It has to be explored, reported, and imagined. Man is no Aristotelian god contemplating all existence at one glance. He is the creator of an evolution who can just about span a sufficient portion of reality to manage his survival, and snatch what on the scale of time are but a few moments of insight and happiness. Yet this same creature has invented ways of seeing what no naked eye could see, of hearing what no ear could hear, of weighing immense masses and infinitesimal ones, of counting and separating more items than he can individually remember. He is learning to see with his mind vast portions of the world that he could never see, touch, smell, hear, or remember. Gradually, he makes for himself a trustworthy picture inside his head of the world beyond his reach.[7]

Much of our world is never experienced directly but, although invisible, at the level of nuclear or cosmic events for example, it may be visualized through film images which, in fact, precede our concrete experiences in many fields. From the early animal locomotion studies of Muybridge and Marey to man's first step on the moon, the human animal, through his unique gift of image-making, is gradually creating, as Lippmann put it, "a trustworthy picture inside his head of the world beyond his reach." This picture is coming to include not only the physical dimensions of our universe but also the psychological dimensions as well.

Sol Worth has pointed out: "While Freud was developing a method that portrayed inner 'reality,' Edison announced that 'finally we have a method of showing the world as it really is.' It is not accidental, I believe, that these opposite solutions to man's search for a picture of reality developed simultaneously."[8]

The important point is that man is coming to realize that he not only can create images, but that he must create his own image of the world and what it means. The security of the stereotyped authority figure, where it was pictured at all, is gone with the wind. Life with father isn't what it used to be, and the day of the autocrat of the breakfast table is past. Because of its power to reify the abstraction, the screen may replace the lectern *if* it does not presume, either in religion or education, to simply replicate the old authority figures and begin "teaching" or "preaching."

What it can do is shed a little light into the dark corners of human behavior and illuminate human aspirations, through the visualization of the commonplace, to a depth that goes far below the surface of the screen image itself. These films of reality, with their beginnings in the Kino-eye, the newsreel, and the documentary, must come from a different breed of film-maker than we have had before, since we now must deal not only with *reality* but also with *relevance.*

It is important, as Antonioni put it, "for a director even more than for other artists, to be committed morally in some way," and "our effort as directors must be that of bringing the data of our personal perceptions of reality into accord with that of a more general experience."[9] It is also important to remember that the film medium is really nothing more than a highly complex symbol system and that we are dealing with symbols and not with three-dimensional reality. The way to bring one's personal experiences into the general experience of the audience is really by creating highly unrealistic symbols which may appear to lack continuity or meaning in many of today's most effective films. Cocteau, for example, tried to create truth in film by "losing the thread." "I mean by this," he said, "that the thread of chronological order would only appear to be lost. In this way perhaps I could employ a more lively and less pretentious method of searching the void."[10] And Alain Resnais, in trying to explain a style also lacking in chronology, plot, or apparent meaning, reported that "most people see only themselves in *Hiroshima* and *Marienbad,* instead of looking at me."[11] The symbols which turned people on proved effective because they stimulated the viewer to make his own connections.

Many films, especially student films which attempt this style, are unsuccessful because of the failure to distinguish between the use of the medium as a shared experience and as personal therapy. Fellini's *8½,* for example, has been regarded by some as the confessional of a lapsed Roman Catholic, but its symbolism makes effective linkage with thousands of other human lives at the same time. The linkage is *relevance,* the method is through *technology,*

131

and the style is *vérité*—or something like it, as seen in the films of William Jersey, Michael Brault, Francis Ford Coppola, and in the work of the National Film Board of Canada in the "Challenge for Change" program.

The expression of truth in everyday reality is not new in the work of the institutions of religion and education or film, either. In *Doctor Zhivago* (from which came a tolerably good film) Boris Pasternak has Nikolai Nikolaievich say:

What has for centuries raised man above the beast is not the cudgel but an inward music: the irresistible power of unarmed truth, the powerful attraction of its example. It has always been assumed that the most important things in the Gospels are the ethical maxims and commandments. But for me the most important thing is that Christ speaks in parables taken from life, that he explains the truth in terms of everyday reality. The idea that underlies this is that communion between mortals is immortal, and that the whole of life is symbolic because it is meaningful.[12]

But the parable needed further explanation and dialogue even for the disciples, and so it is with the film. The films needed, then, must be infused with suggestibility, rich in symbolism, and designed for people—teachers and ministers, for example—who have been schooled in this medium and who are visually literate as well as socially and spiritually awake.

A recent report on the improvement of education in America is based on the fact that the first priority is the improvement of teacher education. "A situational approach is recommended, supplemented by a systematic study of pedagogically relevant aspects of the sociology, anthropology, and linguistics of the inner city, or rural poverty, suburbia, or any part of society from which a pupil comes."[13] The complex behavior involved in the teaching-learning situation, the report continues,

cannot be studied because behavior perishes as it happens and nothing is left to analyze except the memory or a check sheet. . . . To learn to interpret situations they must be held . . . or reproduced at will approximately as they occurred. . . . Until the development of instructional technology, it was difficult to reproduce teaching behavior. But today audio and video recordings of behavior can be made and studied in detail. They make it possible to teach theoretical knowledge of pedagogy in the context of its use as well as in formal courses. . . . To follow this mode of instruction it is necessary to have available an extensive supply of audio and video recordings of home, street, playground, and classroom situations, of committee meetings, and interviews. . . . They should represent the most poverty-stricken and most affluent rural and urban communities, as well as all minority groups. They should also represent all grade levels and teaching procedures such as problem-solving, question-and-answer, and group discussion.[14]

If ministers of the gospel and their leadership expect technology to come to the aid of moral intuition, what is said about film and teacher education in this report should be read with care. "For it is certain," as William A. Bluem writes of television and the church,

that if we are to continue to hold our strength while bringing an often confused and weary populace toward some deeper sense of social and spiritual destiny, these institutions, above all others, must employ the new technology to bring the ancient dreams of mankind toward fulfillment. The growing recognition of this truth has led to a new kind of search. The churches and the broadcasters of America are now engaged in the quest for relevance: each to the individual, each to society, and each to the other.[15]

The kind of films needed will be found among the increasing number of images coming from many sources, if only because their very volume gives us more from which to choose. The best will be simple films, in the tradition of the parable; concrete, yet infused with suggestibility which puts the burden of involvement and interpretation upon the viewer in a way which extends the act of creating the film to the audience itself. These will be "reality" images in the sense suggested in this essay, and they must be relevant. They may break the world up into fragments but they will never be meaningless. They will, in Cocteau's terms, only *appear* to lose the thread, as a "more lively and less pretentious method of searching the void."

Such films are to be distinguished from those, both aboveground and underground, which are formless, fortuitous regressions to the use of film as escapism. The only difference between these films and the escapist films of "Hollywood" is that the latter at least allowed large audiences to get away—often even if they didn't want to go. Many of the current films of the experimentalist, the underground, and the very small, independent producer, are exits for personal escape which might be of considerable psychiatric interest and some therapeutic value, but which have little or nothing to do with either relevance or reality or with film either.

To avoid falling into this new type of screen escapism, the film generation needs to cultivate a sense of disengagement, not from life but from film itself—which is beginning to assume the proportions of life because film is so uniquely suited to, and needed for, the presentation of that increasing part of the "real" world which is out of sight and out of mind. The filmed image we see on the morning television news *is* the world on that particular day. The student film shows his world. It is his and his alone, but now it gradually becomes the world of the student for others.

The worlds of dream and reality, of truth and fiction, often become irretrievably blurred in one gigantic dissolve as in the case of the intercutting of the televised "simulation" scenes of "doubles" of the astronauts actually shown inside a capsule on the ground, with the "live action" scenes of the "stars" who were actually on the moon. Studio and location shots were not distinguished by the general viewing audience, producing a fusable blend of reality and dramatization of a type which may also be compared to Resnais's use of actual newsreel footage of atrocities at Dachau and Auschwitz in *Night and Fog.*

In a violent world, violent images are inevitable. Today's images of horror, destruction, and death in macabre forms dissolve nightmare and reality into representations reminiscent of medieval art. Huizinga points out in *The Waning of the Middle Ages* that the great mysteries of that time seemed to be graspable only when invested with perceptible form and that the consequent horror portrayed in art seemed to be enjoyed by medieval man because he could, at least, understand it.[16] Are the great mysteries and ambiguities of our time being symbolized in the same way— and enjoyed for the same reasons—by modern man? One can only hope that history will repeat itself, that we are on the verge of a great renaissance, that sociological theories of man and calamity are correct, and that we are experiencing a caesura in cultural evolution which is, in fact, at once a death knell and a signal of rebirth. Go to your local movie house regularly, watch "Every Night at the Movies" on television, and find out. Or, in the future, go to your local "Cathedral-Dome"—if predictions growing out of the film experience at Expo '67 and elsewhere materialize.

The writer's strongest recollection of Sunday school is sunlight streaming through a stained glass window picturing Christ standing at a portal with the verse: "Behold, I stand at the door and knock." This image, at the time, seemed to leave a lot to the imagination—enough, at least, to sustain a small boy for several years, especially during the reading of the Scriptures. But this experience may be only dimly related to the effects created by image-bearing environments which schools and churches may come to in the future if the predictions are right.

Vanderbeek, for example, envisions a "movie-drome . . . a spherical dome, onto which simultaneous images of all sorts would be projected, the audience lying down at the outer edge, feet toward the center" in which "each member of the audience will build his own references from the image-flow . . . each individual makes his own conclusions . . . or realizations."[17] It sounds very much like the environment described by Francis Thompson of *N.Y., N.Y.* and *To Be Alive* fame:

Perhaps in some scientifically mystical age that lies ahead, the Cineramas, the Radio City Music Halls and the Planetariums will have evolved into cathedral-like cinemadomes where the mystery and wonders of the universe will be interpreted on the inner walls of vast spheres completely surrounding the viewers. Here the moving image, projected in such a way as to produce three-dimensional effects, would seem to extend out to infinity in every direction. There would be no limiting screen, the image could appear anywhere or everywhere. The artist might swing us out to the stars or down into the depths of the human spirit with all-engulfing hypnotic abstractions in motion. Not long ago such predictions would have seemed overblown and science-fictional. Today they seem the least we can expect.[18]

With the references to terms like "cathedral," "mystery," and "hypnotic abstractions," it is easy to envision such an environment being dug up in ten thousand years or so and being regarded by its excavators with much the same wonder and interest that attended our discovery of the ceremonial cave-images of Altamira. Renoir's characterization of the film studio as a place of the worship of camera and director is translated to the "cathedral-like cinema-dome" as a place of the worship of the image.

There is no value in the development of a Cult of the Image, although we are in danger of developing one or more, complete with high priests and catechism. There is no merit in replacing either the lectern or the pulpit with the screen if its only purpose is to perpetuate the information-dispensing function. There is, on the other hand, little long-range value in the exploitation of multiple-image personal-therapy films in these settings, which is a little like relocating our own navel on the screen—and we certainly have contemplated that long enough.

It is good that young people "groove" with the kinds of films that are being seen today, but this fact alone may or may not have anything to do with reality, relevance, or even art. It has never been difficult for an audience—especially a young audience—to "groove" with a good entertainment film or to become involved in it as a "multisensory," "total," or "simultaneous" experience. But if the experience is nothing more than a "massage" then film may, indeed, be the opiate of the people and we can all repair to a Magic Fingers bed, watch *Petulia* on the late show, while listening to the background music from *The Yellow Submarine,* without having to remember or be responsible for or critical of any of it in the morning. And we are right back where we started when the then-young film rebels and critics and independents assailed the Hollywood Dream Factory for the lack of social conscience expressed in its products and its slogans like "Movies are your best entertainment."

The classic problem of screen education, of course, is involvement on different levels of sensation. It means empathetic engagement as well as critical disengagement; a Brechtian sense of aesthetic distance; the discipline of stepping out of as well as into a situation. Film is a symbol-system and must be looked at in this way when we attempt to relate this medium to reality and to religion. In interpreting these samples of reality there is always the danger of overinterpretation, too. It is entirely possible to talk or teach or preach a film *out* of existence (a characteristic of older film teachers), just as it is possible to talk a film *into* existence (a characteristic of young film-makers and film buffs). Much has been made recently of what is called "visual literacy," "the language" of film, of "grammar" and "syntax" in cinema. Whether, in fact, film can be considered in literary terms at all is highly questionable in the mind of the writer and others.[91] However, there is a need for continuing study of the intricacies of design of this medium and the even more exquisite, exotic, and dramatic effects they produce in the audiences with which they react. Research on the nature of the audience, including studies of subgroups in terms of perceptual abilities and other variables, could help film-makers—not necessarily in terms of enabling them to make better films, but in terms of helping them to understand the little-understood chemistry of image and audience, and to give them a sense of what is "real" on the screen and what is "relevant" in terms of human lives.

Such research, including the use of response systems, can extend the creative act of image-making to those who view as well as those who make films in the same sense that the Czechs combined live and filmed imagery with audience reactions to shape the ending of their presentation *Kino-Automat* at Expo '67. Such research can give producer as well as audience a sense of detachment from the tyranny of the image and time to think about and to shape images with the consciousness that he, through his image-making ability, is shaping himself and others. It may help turn him outward, relieve the visual catatonia evident in many films today, and call his attention to the issues of reality and relevance which need to be expresed on the screen.

We are a generation driven, shaped, and mirrored by images. The important thing seems to be a growing realization that they are images of our own making, and that for the first time in history more people are possessed of the skills, technology, and incentive to tell it as it is on film.

The image, and the image-making drive, is in urgent need of study as a possible evolutionary phenomenon for preparing man for physical and mental changes which even now he may be making upon himself. We must examine the nature and consequences of the excitement generated by film in all its photographic, electronic, and multiple-imaged extensions which explode perceptual traditions and produce "grooving" or even mind-shattering experiences. We must consider the effects of image-environments such as those "cathedral-like movie-domes" envisioned by Thompson and Vanderbeek because they are already upon us. We must examine the nature and conditions of critical disengagement from the film experience; the development of a sense of aesthetic distance, the cultivation of what Dewey refers to as "the passionate intelligence."

The creative challenge as well as the utilitarian promise of the medium is precisely in the fact that film can bridge the gap between a cybernetic model of the world and the reality; between dream and hard fact; between art and science and, as Skrade puts it elsewhere in this book, "serve as a basis for a fruitful dialogue between the church and the world."

## NOTES

1. Stanley Kauffmann, *A World on Film* (New York: Harper and Row, 1966), p. 424.

2. Pauline Kael, *I Lost It at the Movies* (New York: Bantam Books, 1966), p. 247.

3. Henry Miller, *The Cosmological Eye* (Norfolk, Conn.: New Directions Press, 1939), p. 60.

4. Richard Dyer MacCann, *Film: A Montage of Theories* (New York: E. P. Dutton & Co., 1966), p. 16.

5. Georges Sadoul, *The Cinema in Arab Countries* (Paris: UNESCO, 1966), p. 23.

6. MacCann, p. 18.

7. Walter Lippmann, *Public Opinion* (New York: Pelican Books, 1946), p. 20.

8. Sol Worth, "Cognitive Aspects of Sequence in Visual Communication," *Audiovisual Communication Review* 16, no. 2 (Summer, 1968): 122.

9. Michelangelo Antonioni, *Sight and Sound* 31 (Winter, 1963/64): 41.

10. Jean Cocteau, *Paris Album 1900-1914* (London: W. H. Allen, 1956), pp. 14-15.

11. Eugene Archer, "Director of Enigmas," *New York Times Magazine,* March 18, 1962, p. 104.

12. Boris Pasternak, *Doctor Zhivago* (New York: Signet Books, 1960), p. 39.

13. B. Othanel Smith, ed., *Teachers for the Real World* (Washington, D.C.: American Association of Colleges for Teacher Education, 1969), p. 49.

14. Ibid., p. 44.

15. William A. Bluem, ed., *Religious Television Programs: A Study of Relevance* (New York: Hastings House Publishers, Communications Arts Books, 1969), p. 4.

16. Johan Huizinga, *The Waning of the Middle Ages* (New York: Doubleday Anchor Books, 1954), p. 223.

17. Stan Vanderbeek, "Cultural Intercom," in *Sight, Sound, and Society,* ed. David Manning White and Richard Averson (Boston: Beacon Press, 1968), pp. 429-30.

18. Francis Thompson, "More Optic Nerve for the Film Maker," *Art in America* 47, no. 4 (1959): 63.

19. Cal Pryluck et al., *Journal of the University Film Association* 21, no. 2 (Columbus, Ohio: Ohio State University, 1969), p. 4.

# The Contributors

CARL SKRADE is Assistant Professor of Religion at Capital University, Columbus, Ohio. He is an exponent of the value of theological concern with contemporary cinema and a teacher of college theology-films courses.

JOHN C. COOPER is presently Chairman of the Department of Philosophy at Eastern Kentucky University in Richmond, Kentucky. He is the author of *The Roots of Radical Theology, Radical Christianity and Its Sources, The New Mentality,* and *The Turn Right.*

ROBERT W. JENSON is currently Professor of Systematic Theology at the Lutheran Theological Seminary in Gettysburg, Pennsylvania. He is the author of *Alpha and Omega, A Religion Against Itself, The Knowledge of Things Hoped For,* and *God After God.*

JAMES M. WALL is Editor of *The Christian Advocate* and associated with the National Center for Film Study.

WILLIAM HAMILTON is Professor of Religion at New College in Sarasota, Florida, and the author of *The Christian Man, Modern Reader's Guide to the Gospels, The New Essence of Christianity,* and *Radical Theology and the Death of God,* co-authored with Thomas J. J. Altizer.

ANTHONY SCHILLACI, O.P., teaches in the Department of Communication Arts at Fordham University and is Director of Special Projects for the National Film Study Project. In addition to his contributions to such works as *The Saturday Review* and *Listening,* he is the author of *Movies and Morals,* and is preparing a second book, *Mirror, Myth and Morality.*

HARVEY G. COX, JR., is Associate Professor of Church and Society at the Divinity School of Harvard University, and research associate of the Harvard University Program on Technology and So-

141

ciety. He is the author of *The Secular City, On Not Leaving It to the Snake,* and *The Feast of Fools: A Theological Essay on Festivity and Fantasy.*

WILLIAM F. LYNCH, S.J., is currently Writer-in-Residence at St. Peter's College in New Jersey. The author of several books and articles, he is known particularly for his influential works, *Christ and Apollo* and *The Image Industries.*

ROBERT W. WAGNER is Chairman of the Department of Photography and Cinema at Ohio State University. He is a leading academician in his field as well as an award-winning film-maker, and he has authored several articles and studies, including his recent study, "The Generation of Images," for the Federal Commission of Instructional Technology.

*Type,* 10 on 13 and 9 on 10 Times Roman
Display, Optima